N·E·T·S·C·A·P·E™
QUICK TOUR
FOR WINDOWS

ACCESSING & NAVIGATING THE INTERNET'S WORLD WIDE WEB

STUART HARRIS & GAYLE KIDDER

VENTANA
PRESS

Netscape Quick Tour for Windows: Accessing & Navigating the Internet's World Wide Web
Copyright © 1995 by Stuart Harris & Gayle Kidder

Library of Congress Cataloging-in-Publication Data

Harris, Stuart (Stuart H.)
    Netscape quick tour for Windows : accessing & navigating the internet's world wide web / Stuart Harris & Gayle Kidder -- 1st ed.
        p. cm.
    Includes index.
    ISBN 1-56604-244-5
    1. Netscape (Computer file) 2. World Wide Web (Information retrieval system) 3. Internet (Computer network) I. Kidder, Gayle.
TK105.882.H373 1995
025.04--dc20
                                94-47119
                                CIP

Book design: Marcia Webb, Art Director
Cover design: Dawne Sherman, Mike Webster
Vice President, Ventana Press: Walter R. Bruce, III
Developmental Editor: Tim C. Mattson
Product Manager: Clif McCormick
Line Editor: Marion Laird
Technical review: Jonathan Ogden, The Interactive Center
Editorial staff: Pam Richardson, manager; Angela Anderson, Tracye Giles, Nathaniel Mund
Print staff: Wendy Bernhardt, Dan Koeller
Production staff: John Cotterman, manager; Patrick Berry, Cheri Collins
Index service: Dianne Bertsch, Answers Plus
Proofreader: Sue Versényi

First Edition 9 8 7 6 5 4 3 2 1
Printed in the United States of America

Ventana Press, Inc.
P.O. Box 2468
Chapel Hill, NC 27515
919/942-0220   FAX 919/942-1140

Limits of Liability and Disclaimer of Warranty

About the Authors

Stuart Harris is the author of *How to Survive Internet Relay Chat* (irc) (Addison-Wesley) and numerous articles about the Internet in national magazines. He works as an Internet consultant and is leader of his local computer society's Internet special-interest group. He has also been involved in technical editing and TV documentary production. Stuart enjoys communicating complex ideas to a mass audience.

Gayle Kidder is a journalist and editor with 20 years of book, magazine and newspaper experience. Before forming her own media service company, she was employed as a technical editor by the Scripps Institution of Oceanography. She writes regularly for *San Diego Magazine* and the *San Diego Union-Tribune*. She also maintains as a Web page an online column of cultural events for the city of San Diego.

Their joint projects have included TV documentary production, journalism, software product management and, recently, a type of live theater on the Internet. Gayle and Stuart work in the classic "electronic cottage" near the beach in San Diego and are on the Net every day of their lives.

Acknowledgments

We consider ourselves lucky to have had a number of bright and capable Net wizards who cheerfully helped us in the preparation of this book.

Foremost among them is Mark Burgess of the Data Transfer Group in San Diego, a prince among Webmasters, for his unfailing generosity and expert guidance (and for giving us our first copy of Netscape Navigator).

Mike Bowen at CERFnet also provided invaluable assistance on several topics. Phil Hom at Primus Inc. was indispensable in preparing the Macintosh version of the book, for both his Mac expertise and his excellent work in providing the Mac graphics.

Brent Halliburton of Group Cortex, and Steve Sanders of the CyberSpace DataBase BBS, contributed undocumented features. Thanks also go to Gareth Branwyn for giving us, in his forerunning Ventana books about Mosaic, a good model to follow.

Most of all, we'd like to acknowledge each other. Neither of us thinks there's the slightest chance we could have turned this book out on schedule without the other's help and support.

CONTENTS

MENUS, BUTTONS & BARS 27

INTRODUCTION

The first time you wander onto the Internet's World Wide Web is something like entering a magic hall of mirrors. Every time you turn a corner or open a new door, another world opens up for you. As you tunnel your way from one document to the next, deeper and deeper into the maze of information, you begin to wonder if you'll ever find your way home again.

Even more fascinating, one moment you may be in Boston, the next you're in Santa Cruz. Then, at the touch of a mouse, you're off to Tokyo, Stockholm, London or Hong Kong, following your curiosity to your heart's content.

This is the amazing universe that the World Wide Web has created in just a few short years—hundreds of thousands of documents all over the world linked together in a many-filamented web. This new universe is so incredibly diverse and interesting that we are well past the point where any one person comprehends it all. And every day, as more and more people discover the rich resources of the Web and begin to imagine its possibilities, it becomes even richer.

The latest manifestation of this headlong rush toward a new global culture is Netscape Navigator, a software package that's bringing the best of the Internet to the personal computer screens of countless people on every continent of the world. Born as the first commercial offshoot of Mosaic, a U.S. Government product (and using many of the same young brains as designers), Netscape Navigator is a traveling window upon the ever-changing scenery of the Internet.

The Internet itself, which began as a military-scientific project and then branched out to universities, schools and businesses, has now become so democratized that a student in Arkansas can create his or her own "page" on the Web that has standing equal to that of the Smithsonian Institution or the White House visitors' page.

In writing this guide to Netscape, which cannot help but be a guide to the Web as well, we are thinking of our typical reader as reasonably well educated but not necessarily technically inclined. Our target reader may be a teacher or a business person who wants to tap into the resources on the Net but has little time to spend learning complex software programs—the sort of person Netscape was designed for, actually.

He or she may well need help getting Netscape Navigator set up—it's a task comparable in difficulty to programming a modern VCR (which often sends parents to their kids for help). But our prototype reader is, above all, somebody who is ready to explore the Net with us and have some fun while picking up valuable information.

We assume you already have at least an elementary understanding of the Internet, although that may not extend much beyond e-mail. Readers who feel a need for more background on the Internet are advised to pick up one of the many great books on the market now, such as Michael Fraase's *Windows Internet Tour Guide* (Ventana Press), or *The Whole Internet Book* or *Big Dummy's Guide* to the Internet. Excerpts from the latter two can be accessed via Netscape in hypertext versions.

Hardware & Software Requirements

Before we start, there are also some basic hardware and software requirements to be met. "Uh oh," we hear you saying, "Here it comes—

another upgrade." Not necessarily. Naturally, as with most powerful programs these days, the bigger your hard drive and the more RAM you have, the smoother things will be for you.

But if you've got the basics, there's no reason to run out and buy more until you explore the Web and see what kind of information you're likely to want to access. It's perfectly possible to run Netscape with a minimal configuration as long as you're not in a hurry or you're willing to do without the graphic images much of the time. Here's what you need and what's recommended:

- Good: 386 SX with 4mb RAM. Better: 486 with 8mb or more
- Microsoft Windows 3.1 in 386 Enhanced mode
- Good: VGA monitor. Better: SVGA monitor
- Good enough: 9,600 baud modem. Far better: 14,400 baud modem or faster
- A Winsock TCP/IP stack (SLIP/PPP communications software)

In addition, you should make sure you have about 20mb of free hard-drive space. Netscape will need it for creating temporary directories.

And last—but most important—you will need your Internet connection: either a direct connection through your institution or business or a SLIP/PPP connection that can be arranged through a private access provider (more details on this in Chapter 2).

Super-Duper Quick Start

Netscape Navigator is easy to set up and begin using on your own, providing you have a working familiarity with communications software. If your Internet connection is already up and running and you have your copy of Netscape in hand, you can go ahead and install it yourself using the .EXE and setup commands. Once you start to run it, Netscape will take you to its own Welcome page and from there you can follow links to whatever interests you.

Take a look around and enjoy yourself. Soon enough you'll want to know more about some of its special features. Jump ahead to Chapters 3 through 6 to learn how to set up helper applications, use the bookmarks menu, do searches, and use Netscape for FTP, TELNET and newsreading. And since you're a quick learner, we know you'll want to take a look at the "undocumented features" described in Appendix A in the back of this book—things you can do that the user's manual doesn't tell you about.

What's Inside

Chapter 1, "The Net & the Web" provides a brief look at the development of the Web as the newest and fastest-growing segment of the Internet. It explains how the idea of hypermedia in an easy-to-use graphical interface transformed a system once used primarily by the techno-elite into a new democratic forum.

Chapter 2, "Getting Started," tells you how to get your copy of Netscape along with any subsidiary programs you may need. This chapter also gives explicit instructions on downloading via FTP. You'll learn how to set it up once you have it, then we'll take a quick cruise on the Web to demonstrate Netscape's main features.

Chapter 3, "Menus, Buttons & Bars," gives a detailed tour of Netscape's menu items and its easy-to-use buttons. We'll tell you how you can use Netscape's Bookmarks menu to keep track of your favorite Web pages. And we'll guide you in configuring Netscape for reading USENET newsgroups, sending e-mail and doing other things you're interested in on the Internet.

Chapter 4, "Launching Into Cyberspace," begins by taking a closer look at hypermedia on the Web, explaining what you need to play audio files and view movies with Netscape Navigator. Then we'll look at the different kinds of Web documents available for all interests, including online publications, educational resources, museums and art galleries, business sites, travel and recreation and much more. Finally, we'll explain how to use Netscape to do other special applications like FTP, TELNET and reading the USENET news.

Chapter 5, "Making Your Own Web Documents," is a brief primer on designing a Web page. We'll show you visually how we created a simple home page, with easy steps you can follow in designing your own Web document.

Chapter 6, "Special Applications & Sites," explains how to use the Web to search for topics that interest you. Then we'll point you to some prize-winning Web sites and some of our personal favorites to get you started on your own explorations.

Also, we've put in appendices covering some undocumented features and common error messages, as well as a glossary and index for your reference.

Last but not least, we've included a summary of the Netscape Online Companion, which will open up even more adventures accessible only to Ventana customers.

Nothing Stays the Same

When we got our first copy of Netscape Navigator—a Version 9.0 beta release—we were immediately impressed with its superior features, its speed and its friendly interface to dozens of applications. During the writing of this book, Netscape went through three subsequent beta versions to the official Version 1.0 release. We saw a couple of minor screen changes, some diligent bug-chasing, signs of agonizing about Newsgroup functions, and much work on the highly efficient caching system—all that stuff that is supposed to go on behind the scenes without your having to worry about it.

Most likely, additional changes are yet to come, one of which will undoubtedly be a 32-bit version that will be more conservative of Net resources. But we feel fairly confident that you will continue to find this a helpful guide to all the main features of Netscape Navigator, and that all you learn here will be easily translatable to later versions of the software.

The future of the Web is another matter. It is changing so rapidly day by day that it's hard to say where it will all lead six months, a year, two years from now. What is certain is that once you start looking at the Web with Netscape, you'll be as much a part of its future as physicists in Geneva, businessmen in Tokyo and high-school students in Tuscaloosa.

Stuart Harris
Gayle Kidder
San Diego, California

THE NET & THE WEB

The world of personal computing these days is a lot like the Red
Queen's kingdom in "Through the Looking Glass"—everyone seems to
be running faster and faster to stay in the same place. Relatively new
computer users can be forgiven for fearing that they'll never catch up.

If you've gotten as far as acquiring Netscape Navigator and buying
this book, however, cheer up. You can congratulate yourself for being
on the leading edge of the fastest-growing segment of the Internet—the
World Wide Web. As you begin to explore the Web with Netscape
Navigator, the number of resources you'll find there may make you
think this has been going on for a long time. How could you have
missed out for so long? Relax—it's not so. Almost everything you see
now on the Web didn't exist in 1990.

The Web itself wasn't created until 1989. But it did not become
widely accessible to those outside the scientific and academic commu-
nities until the creation of the Mosaic graphical interface in 1993. It was
that event which suddenly made the Web easily available and attractive to hundreds of thousands of computer users around the world.
This set of statistics gives you the idea: in June 1993, there were 130

server sites on the Web; by November 1994, approximately a year and a half later, there were 1,265—a growth rate of more than two a day. Multiply by the number of people logging in at all those sites and you can see where we're going.

Given the rapidly growing interest in the World Wide Web for educational and commercial uses, it's entirely possible that this is your first experience with "that thing" everyone's been talking about for the last few years, the Internet. And you may be wondering, "How does the Internet relate to the Web?" If you're confused about the difference, read on (don't be embarrassed, nobody's looking over your shoulder now, right?).

By the end of this chapter, you should have a fairly clear idea of the world you're entering with Netscape Navigator. By the end of this book, we hope you'll be running alongside the rest of us in the world of computing, trying to keep up with the changes that are hitting us faster every day.

The Internet: Who's in Charge?

Basically, the Internet is the architecture upon which everything else you've heard about hangs. It is nothing more (and nothing less) than thousands of computers all over the world that communicate with each other minute-by-minute over an unbelievably complicated network of cables, fiberoptic filaments and satellite links.

Although it started—back in the Info Stone Age of the '60s—as a creation of the U.S. Government, it's important to realize that the Internet as it exists today belongs to no one country, government or business, no matter how large or powerful, nor is it operated by any single authority.

"So who's in charge?" you might rightly ask. Well, nobody and everybody.

It works something like this: Imagine that you live at the northwest corner of an unbelievably complex network of canals. You need to send a message to somebody at the southeast corner. There may be 1,000 different routes your message could take on its way from one corner to the other, and you have no way of knowing which might be the best—which canals are congested right now, which have been taken out of service for maintenance, which have been blocked by a bus or a large animal falling in. Nevertheless, you can put your message in a bottle, label the bottle "SE" and just toss it into the nearest canal. You can walk away confident that your message will get through as long as there's an agreement between the people who live on this canal system.

The agreement is this: At every canal junction there's a person who knows which routes are blocked in the immediate neighborhood. This person picks up each bottle that comes by, looks at its label, and sends it off down a canal that's relatively free-flowing and going in the right direction. Oh, and one more thing—the bottles are rather small, so if you have a big message you must break it into parts labeled A,B,C... da-da-dah, and put each part in a separate bottle. And there's no guarantee that all of those parts will take the same route or even arrive in sequential order.

You can readily imagine that as long as everyone plays by the rules, your message will get through and be put back together into one piece, even if there is nobody at all who understands the complete network. That key idea, that a network could function without any minute-by-minute overall control by a mastermind, was absolutely revolutionary when it was first suggested. The idea has proven to be much more than just a very good solution to a tough technical problem: it has become a way of thinking that explains a lot about the Internet "culture."

So, when you use Netscape to go and find a document in Stockholm or a picture in Mexico City, and it takes half a minute or so for it all to arrive, you can imagine it as thousands of little bottles, sedately floating your way down a maze of "cybercanals."

The World Wide Web

User-friendliness wasn't an issue back in the '60s when the military and the scientists wove together the first strands of what would become the Internet. If you couldn't enter something like *deroff -w detail.list | tr A-Z a-z | sort | uniq >detail.sorted* at a UNIX prompt, you didn't belong. The people who created, maintained and used the Net were so comfortable with that kind of language, they would use it to talk to each other over the breakfast table. (*"Deroff -w the coffee machine while you're up, would you, dear?"*)

There was absolutely no need for user-friendliness until large numbers of users outside the university system came along. That's why all the great strides down the road to the "ultimate killer app" have been taken in this decade, the '90s.

The World Wide Web is certainly one of those strides. Once it became possible to instantly access hundreds of thousands of documents all over the world, it was only logical to think it possible to skip lightly from one related document to the next without laborious search-and-find operations. The World Wide Web made that possible by means of "hypertext."

Hypertext was an idea waiting to happen ever since the first writer created the first footnote. This is how it works:

Say you're helping your child devise a science project. She's interested in spiders, so that's a start. You go together to the library and find a book on spiders. She finds an interesting section about spiders who eat their own mates or young. That sparks an interest in cannibalism among insects in general. You notice a footnote reference to a book about cannibalism in insects. So you pull down that book, find the appropriate section, and as you're reading you become interested in the curious habits of praying mantises. Here's something you might find in your own back yard and use for an experiment. So you follow yet another bibliographic reference to a book on praying mantises.

If you were using the World Wide Web, all of this running back and forth to library shelves, jumping from book to book, would be made very easy for you. In the initial document on spiders you might see a "hypertext link" to cannibalism in insects—i.e., "cannibalism in insects" would appear highlighted in color in the text. By clicking on the highlighted link, you would go directly to the referenced document. From there, you might follow another hypertext link to "praying mantises." Whenever you find anything you want to keep, you can save it to a file on your own computer. It isn't even necessary to know the location of documents you obtain this way—the address is embedded in the text. Obviously, though, you have to have a starting point.

Now let's say you could click on a picture of a female praying mantis and watch it devour its mate in a short video. You might also press an audio button to hear her crunch, crunch, crunch (if you really wanted to). Now you've gone beyond hypertext to hypermedia.

Once it became possible to transmit not only texts but pictures and audio and movie files, and PC technology reached the stage where they could easily be displayed, the Web—as you can see in Figure 1-1 on the next page—became truly hypermedia.

So we reach the point where we are today, when computer industry titans slug it out with Hollywood moguls on the business pages of newspapers every morning to see who will be the first to deliver to you full-scale home videos, among other things, by a click of the mouse.

What's a Web Page?

You'll hear lots of references to "Web pages" in Net talk. The term can be confusing to a newcomer. A Web page is merely a document designed to be accessed and read over the World Wide Web. It must have an address in a recognized format—the URL, or Uniform Resource Locator—that enables computers all over the world to locate it. Each Web page has its own unique URL. The term "page" arises naturally because of the visual similarity of a Web document onscreen to a magazine page. However, there are important differences to bear in mind, apart from the obvious one: these so-called "pages" have no fixed width, height, weight or physical location. A Web page is actually a data document that has been encoded in ways very similar to typesetting, using a simple code language called HTML (HyperText Markup Language). The code says things like "put a picture here," "make this a header" and "start a paragraph here." It also includes codes that say "put a link here to another document."

All of this code is meant to be interpreted and presented to your screen by a "Web browser." It's your Web browser, as much as the code embedded in the page itself, that actually tells your computer how to display the encoded information—the font to display text in, the screen layout to use—and that in turn is to a certain extent under your personal control. Netscape Navigator is merely one of several Web browsers currently available, albeit one of the newest and most versatile.

The more "traditional" stuff of the Internet—FTP and WAIS and USENET and TELNET and the Gopher—has not gone away. It keeps on growing, and actually much of it can be read by Web software. In the early days of the Web, it could be said (and it was) that the Web was not so much a new part of the Internet as a new way of looking at what was there all the time. With the proliferation of "pages" specifically designed for Web browsing, that no longer holds true. But, certainly, nobody thinks we are anywhere close to being able to do away with the information that is

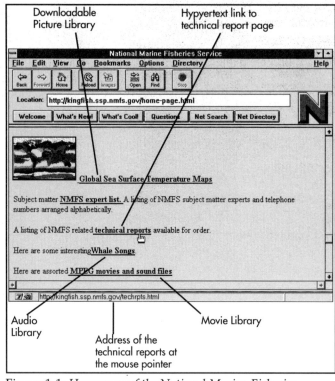

Figure 1-1: *Home page of the National Marine Fisheries Service: a good example of a hypermedia page.*

cataloged in the more traditional ways. On the contrary, there's a clear trend for the graphical Web browsers to include more and more of those other Internet access tools wrapped in ever fancier and friendlier packages. Netscape is squarely in the mainstream of that trend.

Netscape Navigator: Your Window on the Web

When Samuel Morse invented the telegraph, making it possible for stations throughout a railroad's network to get instant information about the running of the trains, people didn't say "Yeah, sure—this may look good right now. But just wait until the telephone comes out. It'll make this collection of wires and keys look like junk overnight." No, obviously the natural reaction to any advance is to rejoice in its benefits and to think that, in the words of the song from *Oklahoma!*, "...they've gone about as fer as they can go."

So it was with NCSA Mosaic, which was such an utterly different view of the Internet that it really seemed to be the be-all and end-all. Wow!! In-line pictures!! Wow!! Instant movies!! Wow!!! Clickable hypertext links!!! WOW!!!!! WOW!!!!! WOW!!!!! It would have sold like hot cakes had it not been the product of a United States Government lab, the National Center for Supercomputing Applications (NCSA) in Illinois. As it is, Uncle Sam does not deal in hot cakes, and the software is free to anyone who can figure out how to download it.

But certain entrepreneurs, who do deal in hot cakes, looked at the "gold rush" of people downloading Mosaic and thought "Hmmmm... maybe if we improved on this and put it on the market...."

Netscape Communications Corporation started by hiring away most of the young computer whizzes who as

Who or What Is Mozilla? Users of Mosaic and lurkers around the USENET groups devoted to the latest developments may have picked up some of the early rumors about a new Web browser called Mozilla. Mozilla was simply the name the young programmers at the University of Illinois at Urbana-Champaign who designed Mosaic gave to their next-generation browser while they were developing it.

The pet name in the programming department was squelched by the marketing department at Netscape Communications Corporation—which was also persuaded by strong-armed attorneys representing the NCSA and the State of Illinois to give up its own first-choice name as Mosaic Communications Corporation. Mozilla survives as an appropriate moniker for the green dragon who welcomes you to his Netscape kingdom when you start up your program.

undergraduates at Urbana-Champaign had designed Mosaic. They set them to work designing a new Web browser that would not just cruise the Web but become an all-inclusive Internet package. Figure 1-2 shows how the design evolved from Mosaic to Netscape. How successful they've been you'll be able to judge for yourself once you get going. At this stage in its development the company welcomes feedback, and by the responses we've gotten to our queries so far, we can report they do pay attention. In the next chapter we'll tell you how to get started with Netscape and join the next wave of the Internet evolution.

The Deluxe Internet Package

Netscape is a full-featured Web browser, which means that it is designed to operate as your principal, if not only, interface with the Internet. If you are already an experienced Internet cruiser, you may have favorite software programs for certain operations, such as reading USENET news or sending and receiving e-mail. You may, of course, elect to continue using these programs. But it will be possible to do most of these operations within Netscape itself. With Netscape you can do all these things:

- access and view Web pages posted anywhere in the world.
- view images (in .GIF, .JPEG and .XBM formats) using Netscape's built-in viewer or a helper application of your choice (like LVIEW).
- play audio and video files using helper applications like WHAM and WPLANY (for audio) and MPEGPLAY and QTWPLAY (for video).
- download and save text, picture, audio and video files to your own computer.
- read and post to USENET newsgroups.

- send e-mail anywhere (but not receive—for that you'll need an accompanying mail program).
- search the Internet using Gopher, WAIS, Archie, Veronica and a whole host of "WebCrawlers."
- download files using FTP.

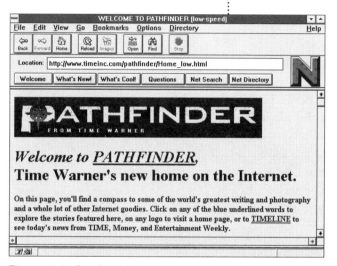

Figure 1-2: *On the right, Mosaic—on the left, Netscape. Can you tell it's the same design team at work?*

Moving On

First, a quick review of the terms we've thrown at you in this chapter. For others you're not familiar with that aren't covered here, please check the Glossary at the back of this book:

The Internet is a worldwide collection of computers that communicate with one another over cables, satellites, optical fibers and phones—literally, the whole hardware mass.

The World Wide Web, or WWW, is a system designed to access documents online over the Internet. It makes it possible to read and exchange text, images, sound and video.

Hypertext and **hypermedia** are what the Web uses to link related documents, allowing the reader to follow connections from one document to the next. Hypermedia is a more appropriate term when links are to audio and video files.

A Web Page is a document designed to be read over the World Wide Web, written with embedded codes for display instructions.

HTML, or HyperText Markup Language, is the coding Web documents or "pages" use to tell a Web browser how to display a text file.

URL, or Uniform Resource Locator, is the address of a file posted on the Web. It tells your Web browser on what machine to find the file and provides the full file pathway.

A **"Web browser"** is a program that allows you to explore the Web. Netscape Navigator is an outgrowth of the NCSA Mosaic, the first graphical Web browser. It is designed not only to read and display Web documents but to be a full-featured interface for most operations you might want to do on the Internet.

Now put down your pencil, turn on your computer and get ready. We're about to take a trip on a silicon chip into the future of the information age.

GETTING STARTED

If you're already Net-savvy, it's a safe bet that Chapter 1 didn't delay you long—and that's fine with us. So now that we're all up to speed, we can start to get organized.

In the style of the latest, most up-to-date software, Netscape Navigator is a breeze to set up, pretty much installing itself on your system. But first you need to pay attention to a few details in getting your system ready to operate.

In this chapter we'll tell you what you need to run Netscape, how to obtain the latest copy of Netscape Navigator by FTP, as well as a number of other applications you might need, and how to install Netscape on your computer and set basic preferences. Then we'll fire up the engines, give you a quick look at the Web pages where you can learn more about Netscape and the Web, and launch you on your first round-the-world cruise on the World Wide Web.

Necessary Connections

To run Netscape Navigator you will need either a direct Internet connection (such as that used by universities, government offices and some businesses) or you will need to set up a SLIP (Serial Line Internet Protocol) or PPP (Point-to-Point Protocol) connection with a private provider. These are getting easier and cheaper to get every day.

Many online access providers now offer a complete kit of all the software, preconfigured for their system, that you need to get set up on the Web. The kit may include Netscape Navigator and a TCP/IP stack to make your connection to the Internet. If you're shopping for a provider, you might ask about this and, all other things being equal, choose one who will go this extra step for you.

Peter Kaminski's List of Internet Service Providers You can obtain an up-to-date list of Internet service providers by sending an e-mail message to info-deli-server@netcom.com with the message **Send PDIAL.** If you're currently not on the Net, have a connected friend get the list for you.

If you choose a provider that does not offer this service, there's still an easy solution: several popular book/software packages such as *The Windows Internet Tour Guide* (Ventana Press) and the Internet Membership Kit (Ventana Media) provide all the software you need for a SLIP/PPP connection.

If you're putting it all together yourself, you will need a little patience. It sometimes takes several trial-and-error attempts at setting things up before you have your communications package running smoothly. Your sysadmin (if you have one) will be your best advisor through this process—he or she knows the system better than you'll ever need to. It is outside the scope of this book to go into the details of configuring your system for communications since there are too many variations to cover. But we will try to point you in the right direction for what you'll need.

Your TCP/IP Stack

If you are running under Windows 3.1, you'll need a TCP/IP stack, also called a Winsock, to make your connection to the Internet. This program acts as an intermediary—dialing your access provider and managing the data exchange between your computer and the Internet.

If you're using Windows NT or have used Mosaic, you should already have a Winsock that will work for Netscape and you can skip this section. If you're setting up for the first time, you can get everything you need online by anonymous FTP. If you're unfamiliar with the process, we'll explain later.

One TCP/IP package that Netscape recommends is NEWT—the communications part of an Internet package called Chameleon Sampler. Chameleon is a very attractive Windows package that includes a mail manager and FTP and TELNET programs. We have, however, found it to be a bear to configure. If your access provider is willing to give you a preconfigured version, though, take it.

Chameleon is commercial software, which can be found packaged with some Internet books or kits. To purchase a full version, direct e-mail inquiries to **sales@netmanage.com**. A "starter" version, however, which includes NEWT, is available by FTP at

ftp.cyberspace.com/pub/slip/Windows/chameleon

(Ignore the instructions in the README.TEXT, which are only of interest to Cyberspace clients.)

A simpler and highly reliable TCP/IP stack, although not as complete a package, is Trumpet Winsock, a shareware product developed by Peter Tattam of the University of Tasmania. The latest version as of this writing is Trumpet Winsock 2.0. There are two files you should download:

twsk20b.zip and **winapps2.zip**.

The Ventana Visitors Center   Ventana offers an Online Companion for the *Netscape Quick Tour* as part of the Ventana Visitors Center. The Online Companion offers all the software mentioned in the *Quick Tour*, with the latest versions accessible as soon as they are made available, along with version change notes. There is also an online guide that will provide you with quick access to Internet resources related to this book. The Netscape Quick Tour Online Companion will help make this book dynamic, up-to-date, and continually useful.

The Ventana Visitors Center can be accessed as follows:

FTP   ftp.vmedia.com
WWW   http://www.vmedia.com/vvc/index.html
e-mail   info@vmedia.com (In body of message,
              type **send help**.)

If you already have a Web browser running, access the Netscape Quick Tour Online Companion at

http://www/vmedia.com/netscapeqt.html

Two locations where you can get it are

ftp.utas.edu.au/pc/trumpet/winsock

ftp.sunet.se=/pub/pc/windows/mirror-cica/ winsock

The current TCP/IP stack for Windows for Workgroups 3.11 is available from Microsoft's anonymous FTP site. The file is **WFWT32.exe** and the address is

ftp.microsoft.com/peropsys/windows/public/ tcpip

One last thing: compressed files will have to be unzipped to install on your system. If you don't already have PKUNZIP, the popular DOS utility for unzipping compressed files, you can get it at

ftp.epas.utoronto.ca/pub/pc/util/pkz204g.exe

For instructions on downloading files via FTP, see "Downloading Netscape," coming up.

Downloading Netscape

Netscape is available via the Internet directly from Netscape Communications Corporation or any of a number of mirror sites (see the "Mirror Sites" sidebar ahead). According to the license agreement for Version 1.0, the software is free for use by educational and nonprofit institutions and for an unspecified evaluation period for all others. You can get information on registering your copy and getting support once you have Netscape installed.

What's All This About 16-bit and 32-bit? If you previously ran Mosaic 2.0alpha6 or higher, you had to install Win32s, a freeware add-on to Windows 3.1 for 32-bit operation. (Windows NT and Windows 95 are already 32-bit.) You won't need this for Netscape, but don't throw it away. There's every reason to believe that a 32-bit application is in the works—perhaps quite soon. (Mosaic started in 16-bit mode and grew up quickly.)

So what does all that mean anyway? Imagine a bridge into a major hub city with 16 toll booths, eight for each direction. In the off-peak hours, 16 toll booths may be adequate to handle the traffic, but come rush hour, the booths get pretty congested and it takes a lot longer for everyone to get through. Expand to 32 booths and everyone's going to get through faster and things will run a lot smoother.

That's a fair analogy for the difference between 16-bit and 32-bit operation. The package of information that gets through at any one time is twice as large. Using 16-bit software is adequate to do the job, but when the Internet's busy—and it's getting harder to find a time when the Internet isn't busy—traffic is going to be considerably held up. 32-bit applications are more compact, more fluent, generally faster—and definitely the wave of the future.

You can get a copy of the software by anonymous FTP with either a DOS or Windows-based communications program. If you already have a SLIP/PPP account and have been using Mosaic, you can download Netscape using Mosaic's FTP feature, but it probably won't be as fast as using conventional FTP. (This is just one way that Netscape has surpassed Mosaic—its own FTP procedure is a delight to use.)

Note: You can obtain Netscape using a dial-up shell account and set it up on your computer. However, in order to use Netscape with anything other than local files (files in your own computer or network), you will need a SLIP/PPP connection or a direct Internet connection.

Using Traditional FTP on a Dial-Up Account

If you have a regular dial-up shell account, you can obtain Netscape using FTP or ncftp. You can try accessing Netscape Communications Corporation directly first to download from there. But in all likelihood, due to heavy use, you'll be referred to one of the other sites where Netscape is also available. You can save time by choosing a mirror site now from the list in the sidebar on mirror sites. We'll use Netscape's FTP site for our example, but you can substitute any of the addresses listed.

1. Use your regular communications program to log onto your account.

2. At the prompt, type **ftp ftp.mcom.com** (or **ncftp ftp.mcom.com**).

If you already have an FTP or ncftp prompt, you'll type **open ftp.mcom.com**

Mirror Sites to Obtain Netscape Mirror sites are other computer centers which by agreement make the same software available publicly for downloading. Any changes made to the main site are soon "reflected" by the mirror sites. Here's a list of sites where Netscape is currently available. We suggest you choose one of these for your downloading procedure:

ftp.digital.com/pub/net/infosys/Netscape
ftp.uu.net/networking/info-service/www/netscape
src.doc.ic.ac.uk/packages/Netscape
unix.hensa.ac.uk/pub/netscape
ftp.luth.se/pub/infosystems/www/netscape
ftp.riken.go.jp/pub/WWW/netscape
ftp.adelaide.edu.au/pub/WWW/Netscape

For the best access, you should normally choose a site close to you. If you don't know what the addresses mean, simply avoid suffixes like *uk* and *au* for United Kingdom and Australia, for instance. On the other hand, we've found accessing Australia or Japan when it's the middle of the night there to be a good strategy sometimes.

Note: If you're using a mirror site, you'll use the part of the address before the first slash.

3. Enter and you'll soon be connected to the server at Netscape Communications Corporation. If you're using FTP, log onto the remote system as "anonymous" and give your e-mail address as the password. If you're using ncftp, you won't have to (it's done for you).

4. Change the directory to the place where the current version of Netscape is available. (Everything that follows the first slash in the FTP address is the directory structure.) At Netscape Communications Corp. the full address is

ftp.mcom.com/netscape/windows

so the command would be **cd netscape/windows.**

With some of the longer addresses in the mirror sites, finding the right directory may be a bit more labyrinthine (they sometimes change). Just remember that at any point in the directory structure, you can ask for a list of files or subdirectories by using the ls command. The command ls -l will give you a fuller description of contents, which sometimes helps in figuring out what you want.

5. Once you've accessed the right directory, the next screen you may see is a fairly fearsome warning against downloading Netscape for exportation to countries where the U.S. bans technology exports. By now you may be feeling like a spy, but don't worry. Everything you're doing is perfectly legal as long as you're not an enemy national.

Type **ls**, press Enter and you'll see a list of files available for downloading, which will include the following:

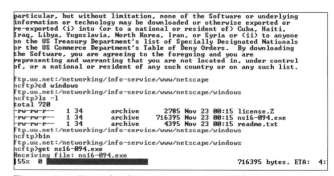

Figure 2-1: *Downloading Netscape the old-fashioned way—using ncftp in a UNIX shell.*

license.Z	ns16-100.exe	readme.txt

You needn't bother downloading the license agreement or the README file, since both will come with the main software package. See Figure 2-1.

6. You'll need to tell the host computer you want the file downloaded as a binary file. Type **bin** and Enter. Then type

   get ns16-100.exe

(or whatever the latest version is called). The file will begin to transfer to your local host computer. When it is done transferring, type **quit**.

7. If you're on a dial-up account, you will have to download the file once again from the host computer to your own home computer. Download the file into a temporary directory on your system. If you rename the file when you download it, be sure to keep the .exe file extension.

Note: The procedure for downloading a file from the host computer to your own machine may differ according to the communications program you're using and the type of service you have. If you don't know how to do that, consult your communications program manual or ask your sysadmin.

More Useful Booty: WINFTP If you don't have a Windows-based FTP program and would like one to use with your SLIP/PPP connection, you can obtain a very good one, WINFTP, by anonymous FTP at

ftp.sunet.se:/pub/pc/windows/mirror-cica/ winsock

The program is called WINFTP.ZIP. Use the procedures outlined above to download it to your system.

Using a Windows-Based FTP Program

If you already have your SLIP/PPP connection and your TCP/IP software installed, you can use a Windows-based FTP program such as Chameleon or WINFTP to download Netscape from Netscape Communications Corp. or one of the mirror sites mentioned previously in this chapter.

We'll use Netscape Communications Corporation's FTP site for our example, but you can substitute any of the addresses listed.

1. Log onto your account in the usual manner.

2. Launch the FTP program and set it for a binary file transfer.

3. Type **ftp.mcom.com** in the appropriate box for Host. (If you're using a mirror site, the Host name will be the part of the address before the first slash.)

Set your program to log in anonymously (or type **anonymous** in the User name box and your e-mail address in the Password box).

4. Choose the OK button or whatever the command is to establish the FTP connection. You'll soon be connected to the server at Netscape Communications Corporation (or your mirror site).

5. Once you are connected to the remote site, make your way through the directory structure to the appropriate directory. At Netscape Communications Corp., this is **/netscape/windows**. With any of the mirror site addresses, everything that follows the first slash in the FTP address is part of the directory structure. With a very long address, this is something like winding your way down through a multistory subterranean parking facility looking for a parking spot. Eventually you'll see a list of files available for downloading, which will include the following:

license.Z   **ns16-100.exe**   **readme.txt**

You needn't bother downloading the license agreement or the README file, since both will come with the main software package.

6. Choose the appropriate version of Netscape and transfer it to a temporary directory on your computer using your program's Copy command. See Figure 2-2. Exit the remote site and you're ready to install Netscape on your computer.

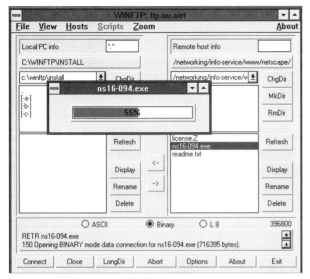

Figure 2-2: *Netscape coming down by WINFTP.*

Unpacking & Installing Netscape

If you followed instructions earlier, you will have the Netscape file you downloaded from the Internet installed in a temporary directory. The file you downloaded is an executable file, which means that when you type the name of the file (you needn't add the .EXE extension), it will automatically install Netscape, creating the necessary files and placing them on your system. It will also create a Windows program item for you.

1. Type the executable command. For the Version 1 that we downloaded in the example above, the file is **ns16-100.exe**, so type this:

    ns16-100

Note: If you change the name of the file when you download it to your system, be sure to keep the .EXE extension. You can then execute the program with the new name you gave it.

Netscape will begin to create the files it needs. You'll see a progress report on the screen as it extracts the necessary files. When it's done, you will see a list of several files it created, one of which is SETUP.EXE.

2. Now type **setup**

The setup program will next open Windows and you will see a Netscape Setup window, then a Welcome screen. Choose "continue" to proceed with setup.

3. You'll be prompted to choose a directory, which must be a different directory than the one your temporary setup files are in. The default directory is C:\NETSCAPE, which the setup program will create for you. If you want a different directory, you can type that in now.

4. Next you will be prompted to choose a Windows program group to add Netscape to.

5. When the setup program finishes, you will be left in Windows, ready to launch Netscape—provided you have the necessary supporting software we suggested earlier. You can delete the files in the temporary directory, which are no longer necessary. All of the important files have been transferred to your new directory, along with some new ones the setup program created.

Setting Basic Preferences

You should be able to start up and begin operating Netscape immediately. However, be aware that some functions on the menu, such as Newsgroups and mail operations, will not work until you first make the appropriate settings.

To set up initial settings for things like mail, newsgroups and helper applications, choose the Options menu item, then Preferences. The pop-up window that appears has five different categories for things you can set. (See Figure 2-3.) We'll talk more about some of these later, but here are some helpful initial settings:

Mail: In the Mail and Proxies dialog box, put in your mail host and your personal e-mail address. If you don't know the name or full pathway of your mail host, ask your sysadmin.

Newsgroups: Put in the name and full pathway of your NNTP news host in the dialog box for Directories, Applications and News. If you don't know it, ask your sysadmin.

TELNET access: If you have software you normally use to access TELNET, specify the appropriate path, and the command to execute it, in the Directories, Applications and News dialog box.

Helper applications: For displaying audio and video files, Netscape uses "helper applications." If you have other software you use for

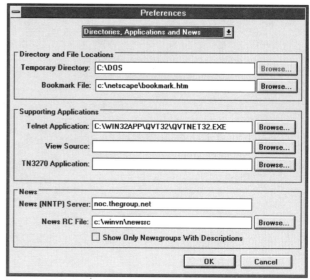

Figure 2-3: *One of Netscape's five Preferences dialog boxes.*

playing movies or audio files, you'll need to let Netscape know by entering the name of the application in the appropriate place in the Helper Applications dialog box. (See Chapter 4.)

Note: Netscape has its own image viewer that it uses by default, so you will be able to operate Netscape and view World Wide Web pages without an accessory image viewer like LView. With LView the image quality may be somewhat better and you will be able to store and manipulate images in ways that Netscape does not allow. You will not be able to play movie clips without a video application.

Netscape Quick Peek

Ready to set sail on your first cruise of the World Wide Web? Here's what you should have done already:

- Set up your local SLIP/PPP connection to the Internet.
- Installed a TCP/IP stack on your system.
- Downloaded and installed Netscape.

Now let's go.

1. First open Windows, if you're not already there.

2. Using your TCP/IP stack (Trumpet Winsock, NEWT or whatever you have), dial your account and log in. Once you're connected and SLIP is enabled, you can minimize the program on Windows.

3. Start Netscape by clicking on the icon or by using the run command.

Netscape Vs. Mosaic: Netscape's superior features:

- A nice big STOP button that really does abort page loads.
- Much better progress reporting as a large page or file loads.
- Something you can watch as the in-line GIFS are forming.
- Built-in image viewers.
- Free choice of home page.
- Images button to reload page showing in-lines.
- More keyboard keys that work reliably.
- Built-in newsreader.
- Excellent FTP management.
- Drag-and-drop HTM file to Netscape content area.

The first time you run Netscape, you will be presented with the current license agreement and be asked to "Accept" its terms before continuing. Read, reflect and act accordingly.

As its first act, Netscape will take you to its own Welcome page at Netscape Corporation. As it searches for its connection, you'll see the little logo on the top right side of the screen activate; then you'll see the page-loading information on the bottom of the screen. All of this means that you're already sailing the net!

Note: If the logo stays active and nothing's happening on the bottom of the screen except for a message saying "Trying to locate host..." you've got a connection problem. You may have to talk to your sysadmin or other technical support source to get it straightened out.

The Welcome page gives you information on the latest developments with Netscape (see Figure 2-4). You'll be given an opportunity to register your copy of Netscape, a good idea if you want to be apprised of updates.

Just above the main screen (your "Web TV") you'll see the directory buttons. Each of these takes you to another information page about Netscape. Probably the most useful of these directory buttons is Questions. Click on this button and you'll go to a directory of FAQs (frequently asked questions) about Netscape. If you've got any problems to solve or questions about setup, this is the place where you're likely to find the answers.

You can follow any links by clicking on the highlighted words on any page. They'll take you to the next page of information on that topic.

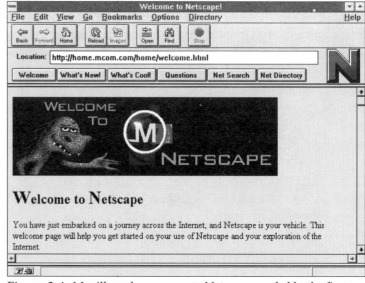

Figure 2-4: *Mozilla welcomes you to Netscape: probably the first Web page you will see.*

After accessing and reading a page, you can "back out" of it by choosing the Back button from the toolbar on the top of the screen. This will return you to the previously displayed page. If you're several pages along, you can keep backing out until you get to your original starting point. Netscape keeps a short list of where you've been—a little trail of bread crumbs through the forest—so you can follow your path back. Or choose the Home button on the toolbar and you'll return immediately to the Welcome page—unless you're ahead of the class and have already figured out how to set your own home page.

Using URLs

Now let's go some place exciting and have some fun. Click on Open on the toolbar and a long rectangular Open Location window will pop up. This is like jumping into a taxi in a strange town. Like most taxi drivers, this one expects you to know where you want to go. You must enter an address in the window.

Every Web page has its own address, its URL (Uniform Resource Locator). The window is extra-long because all the addresses on the World Wide Web are long. And, as you'll find out, addresses must be entered just right.

If you already have an address of a Web site you'd like to check out, you can enter it now. Then click on the Open button and you're on your way. If like a lot of people new in town you don't know any addresses yet, pick one that interests you from our list at the back of this book—or try the one shown in Figure 2-5:

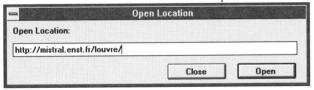

Figure 2-5: *The Open Location dialog box: We're off to Paris!*

Click on Open *et voila! Bienvenue au WebLouvre!* You have just docked along the Seine in Paris, France, where you are ready to take a tour of one of the most famous art museums in the world. See Figure 2-6.

Besides the fun of traveling halfway around the world in a few seconds, this Web site is a good one for illustrating the ways Web pages work. You'll notice a menu of things you can do from this Welcome page—such as a tour of famous paintings in the Louvre, (including the ability to follow links to information about various artists), a visit to a special exhibit, and any of several sightseeing tours of Paris. Choose any one item from this menu by clicking on the highlighted text and you'll go to another page of options.

Many of the pages contain small photos. You'll see blue borders around the pictures, just like the highlighted text links. This means you can click on the pictures and obtain larger versions of them to display on your screen. (The initial pictures are deliberately kept small so that they won't take a long time to load.) If you've got your audio system configured, you can also visit the auditorium and choose a little music to play while you stroll. Ah Paris! Wander around Paris with Le WebLouvre and soon you'll be feeling like a sophisticated citizen of the Web.

Figure 2-6: *This page by Nicholas Pioch has won many design awards—and rightly so.*

Plugging Into Your Own Home Page

If you like Le WebLouvre, you might like to live here for awhile. In the world of the Web anything is possible. You could choose to make Le WebLouvre your home page, so that every time you start up Netscape you'll go straight to Paris.

Practically speaking, this probably isn't a great idea. Le WebLouvre's Web pages are such big files, and so rich in images, that you've probably noticed it takes a little while for them to load (unless you're lucky enough to be on a high-powered computer system).

But you can set up any page you choose as your home page, and you'll probably want to soon. Mozilla does get a little tiring after a few sessions. Many access providers have their own home pages with local information for their clients. If yours does, this might be a good place to start. Or you might prefer to go straight to some useful data page you've found.

To set your home page, choose Options from the menu at the top of the screen. From the pull-down menu, choose Preferences to get a dialog box with a pop-up window offering several options. Scroll to Styles (if it's not already displaying that window) and click or Enter. This dialog box gives you the option of changing things like fonts and display options—you might want to play around with these later.

One of the options asks whether you want to start Netscape with a blank page or a chosen home page location. Choose the Home Page Location radio button then enter the address of your chosen home page in the window. Click okay and exit. You now have a new home page that will appear every time you start Netscape, or when you click on the Home button on the toolbar—until you change it again.

Later we'll show you how to devise your own home page that includes bookmarks to all your favorite sites so you can access them quickly.

Moving On

If you had a little trouble getting your SLIP/PPP connection to work, you're not alone. It seems to be a fact of life that computer communications don't work right the first time. Often they need a few rehearsals before they're ready to perform properly.

By now, though, all that downloading and installation should be behind you and you're home free. We've already introduced you to some of the features of Netscape. Next we'll tour the screen and take you through it menu by menu and button by button.

MENUS, BUTTONS & BARS

Using Netscape Navigator is a breeze, since most operations are self-explanatory. Once you're all up and running, you should have no problem starting to explore the World Wide Web on your own. Everything you really need is built in, so even without any fancy helper applications, you won't need anything extra till you're ready to tackle some gee-whiz, technowizard sites. But because the program has so many extra features, it may take you a while to discover all the things Netscape can do for you.

One of the things you'll notice as you become familiar with Netscape is that there's almost always more than one way to do something. There's a reason: when you become proficient at navigating your way around the Web, you may decide that it would be nice to have a bigger window for viewing documents. You can unclutter your screen and enlarge it by about one quarter by making the toolbar and directory buttons—and even the URL location window—disappear. Everything you want to do can then be done using the considerably less-screen-hogging menu bar—or even the keyboard, if you and your mouse are not inseparable.

We don't advise getting rid of the buttons and bars until you become familiar with all of the functions, however, and for one very good reason. Whenever a toolbar button is available to perform a function (see Figure 3-1), that's the simplest and fastest way to do it. This isn't always the case with the directory buttons, which are largely introductory. For that reason we'll start our walkaround of the screen with the toolbar, move on to the menu bar, and end with the directory buttons. If there is more than one way of doing a particular function, we'll give you the alternatives, including menu items and keyboard commands. The recommended best way will be highlighted with asterisks.

Finally we'll show you how to set up your bookmarks list to your best advantage—a tricky task, but we'll do it step by step. Then we'll take a second look at the options available to you under Preferences, so you can customize Netscape to run the way you want it to and get the most from your helper applications for audio and video files.

The Toolbar: Navigating in Netscape

The toolbar strip is normally quite prominent (those big buttons are great if you're not all that dexterous with the mouse). You can choose the way you want the toolbar button displayed under the Options/Preferences/Styles dialog box. If you want to gain some screen size, you can make it go away altogether by unchecking Show Toolbar in the Options pull-down menu.

Figure 3-1: *The eight much-used toolbar buttons.*

Back

Takes you back to the last Web page you were viewing. The page will almost always come from your cache, and so will load very quickly. If you are on the first page of the session or at the beginning of your history list, this button and the menu option are both grayed out.

Other Ways of Doing This
Menu Go/Back

Other Ways of Doing This
Menu Go/Forward

Forward

 Takes you one page forward in the history list (the record of your recent travels that Netscape keeps for you; see Figure 3-13 and the explanation under "Menu Go/History"). Obviously this has no meaning unless you have already done at least one Back move. Like Back, the page comes from your cache and will load quickly, and if you are at the end of your history list, the button will be grayed out.

Other Ways of Doing This
Menu Go/Home

Home

 Takes you immediately to your home page. At first the default will be the Netscape Welcome screen. Define whatever home page you want in Preferences/Styles in the Main menu.

Other Ways of Doing This
Menu View/Reload; Ctrl-R; Alt-V/R

Reload

At times of heavy-duty use of Netscape, or any other Web browser, you may find curious things happening to your pages: Typefaces will break up; in-line .GIFS will go all crumbly; text will go into "greek" or get partly overlaid by pictures. These are signs that whatever arrangements your computer has for caching are overloaded, and now is when you need the Reload feature. It basically says "This page is a dog's breakfast—let's start over."

One other situation in which you might use this feature is when you are trying to view the source code of a page. If the page is coming from your cache, the source code will not be accessible. You will get an error message, and Reload will solve the problem.

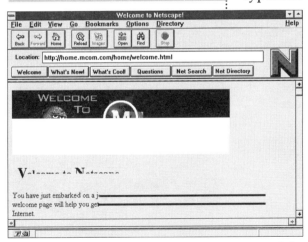

Figure 3-2: *This page really needs to start over: a job for the Reload button.*

Images

 Unless you have lots of computer power at your command (and time to kill), it's a good idea to run Netscape in the "no in-line .GIFS " mode on a day-to-day basis (uncheck Auto Load Images on the Options pull-down). It saves time downloading those page decorations that may not add a whole lot. But even the most hurried Web explorer occasionally wants (or needs) to see what the page designer intended. So, take this option, and Netscape redraws the exact same page that's already onscreen , but this time showing all the in-line images.

Other Ways of Doing This
Menu View/Load Images
Ctrl-I
Alt-V/I

Open

 This is what you do if you know exactly what URL you want to go to but it isn't yet in your bookmark list for handy fly-by-mouse. There's a first time for everything.

A dialog box appears, with a nice L-O-O-O-OOO-ONG window for you to input the URL. Even if your URL reaches the end of the box, you can still keep on entering. Be aware that URL addresses are case-sensitive and have to be entered exactly. Option buttons are Open, to tell Netscape to go where you just told it (Enter also works) and Close, if you think better of it. The key combination Alt-F4 also acts as Close.

You can move the dialog box elsewhere on the screen (even outside the main Netscape window) with the mouse or by clicking on the control button, then using the arrow keys.

Other Ways of Doing This
Menu File/Open Location
Ctrl L
Alt-F/L

Find

 Lets you find a word or string in the current document. Don't confuse this with searching the Web for topics. What it does do is let you search a document you've accessed for a particular string—say "sea turtles" in a document on endangered species. You can make the search case-sensitive if you like.

Other Ways of Doing This
Menu Edit/Find
Ctrl-F
Alt-E/F

Stop

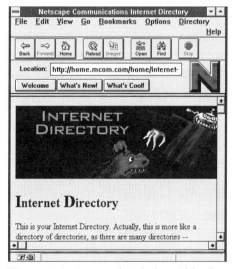

As long as the stop button is showing red, aborts loading of a document—usually used because loading is taking too long. Leaves you with a partially loaded page that can be viewed and used normally so far as it goes. At the bottom of the partial page, Netscape thoughtfully adds the reminder "Transfer interrupted!"

Mosaic Users Note: Clicking on the animated logo—the manner of stopping a load in Mosaic—will do you no good. Instead of stopping a load, it actually takes you to Netscape Communications Corporation's home page.

Main Menu Bar

File	Edit	View	Go	Bookmarks	Options	Directory		Help

Figure 3-3: *Netscape's eight-item menu bar.*

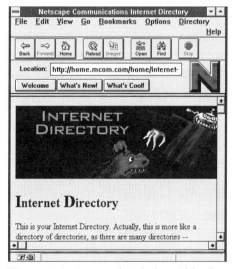

Figure 3-4: *As you shrink the width of the Netscape window, you begin to lose a few buttons....*

Figure 3-5: *...but all the Menu options remain available no matter how thin you make it.*

File

New Window   Ctrl-N or Alt-F/N

Select this option and you get a whole new Netscape
to play with. This is a very neat feature, taking
advantage of the bandwidth of a SLIP connection to
bring you multitasking. Say you start Netscape off
pulling down a page that you know is going to take

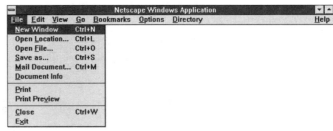

Figure 3-6: *The ten options in the File pull-down menu.*

time. Instead of drumming your fingers and whis-
tling ten bars of "The Yellow Rose of Texas," you could open another
window and do something else. It's also useful if you want to follow a
link but keep the original page up at the same time. (See Figure 3-7.)

The maximum number of windows you can open is set in your
netscape.ini file (Max-Connections=). Four is a reasonable number; six
would be getting greedy (and impossibly slow, on most systems). Ctrl-
Tab switches you between windows.

Open Location...   Ctrl-L or Alt-F/L

Brings up the long dialog box for you to enter the URL address of a
Web page you want to go to.

Open File...   Ctrl-O or Alt-F/F

This option is very different from the Open Location option. If you try
it, you'll see it leads to a typical Open File dialog box, and the List Files
Of Type pull-down defaults to "*.htm." This might give you a clue as to
the purpose of this feature, since a file with the extension .htm is
probably a text file written in the special code known as HTML, or
HyperText Markup Language. We'll be explaining HTML in Chapter 5
of this book—but for now, all you need to know is that this option
brings an HTML file from your own computer (or local network) into

> **Other Ways of Doing This**
> ***The toolbar Open button
> Direct entry to the URL window.

Netscape where it will be interpreted as a Web page. This is the so-called "local mode" used all the time by Web page authors using Netscape as an authoring tool.

 HOT TIP — — — — — — — — — — — — —

Did you know you can place a local .htm file in the Netscape window by drag-and-drop from the File Manager? You can—it's just a matter of arranging the windows appropriately.

Save As...   Ctrl-S or Alt-F/S

This is how to save a Web document that you want to preserve, manipulate, send someone for Christmas, plagiarize or feed to your dog. It leads to the usual Windows File Save dialog box.

There's a surprise in store for you the first time you do this. The document you save will NOT look like it did on the screen. It will have stuff like <DL></DL> all embedded in it. Those are the HTML codes that create the look of the page. Once you save it you will be able to display it as a local file using the Open File option.

Since this is the Web, what you are saving may not be text at all—it may be a picture, a sound, a movie. Make sure it has the right file extension for the file type.

Save Link As...

This is not really a menu option but it's a useful feature and this seems a good place to explain it. Netscape lets you save a page to a file without actually displaying it at all. This could be quite a time-

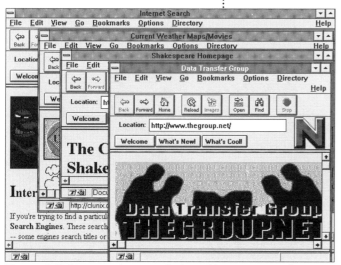

Figure 3-7: *Netscape lets you do four things at once, if you're so inclined.*

saver if it's a complex document and the Net is being crabby, as it often is (especially on Fridays when every university computer comes up for weekly maintenance). Place your cursor on the hypertext link to the page, then hold down the Shift key as you click the mouse button. You will be led straight to the Save As... dialog box, and Netscape should be clever enough to know whether you are saving text, a picture, a movie or audio.

Mail Document...   Ctrl-M or Alt-F/M

This might well have been put on a different menu or button and just called Netscape's "outgoing mail" feature, for that's really what it is—and a very nice one too.

When you select "Mail Document" a large dialog box appears which is basically an e-mail blank ready for you to fill out. The Subject box defaults to the name of your current document, and a nice big Include Document Text button is available. But you can easily ignore all that and simply send a general message (for instance, comments to a Web page author).

If you *do* want to include the text of your current page, you'll find that a piece of cake too. Simply click on the button and the text is imported into the message body window in a flash. Each line starts with the > symbol, like a conventional e-mail quote. (See Figure 3-8.) Also, all of the HTML codes are edited out. There's no perfect way to do this, but the other neat thing about this feature is that you can put a cursor in there and edit away to your heart's content.

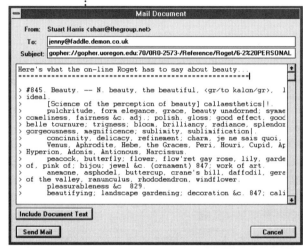

Figure 3-8: *An entry from the online thesaurus turned into e-mail in a flash.*

You can also drop into the message body anything in the Clip-board—an extract from a Web page that you've previously out-lined and done "Edit/Copy" (Ctrl-C) with, for instance. Simply place your cursor where you want the text and press Ctrl-V. When you're done, there are buttons for "Send" and "Cancel."

Warning: Your message is going nowhere if you have not told Netscape about your e-mail arrangements in the Preferences box Mail and Proxies.

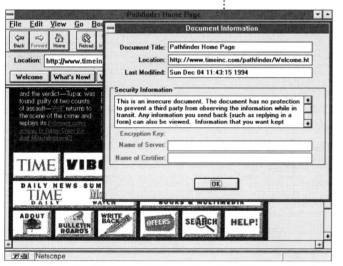

Figure 3-9: *The Document Information box tells you about security.*

Document Info   Alt-F/D

Choosing this item brings up the document informa-tion box (see Figure 3-9), giving information about the history and security of the current page.

Print   Alt-F/P

Choosing this brings up the standard Windows Print dialog box, enabling you to change your printer setup or, more often, just go ahead and print. The page will print more or less as it looks—not as a source docu-ment. (If you want to print source code, use File Save, get the file in a Notepad window and use Notepad's print function).

Print Preview   Alt-F/V

Netscape's print preview facility is very thorough. A layout routine does its best to figure out how to present the page given the limitations of your printer. It then presents you with a picture of how the page will look, and offers buttons for (P)rint, (N)ext Page, Pre(v) Page, (T)wo Page, Zoom (I)n, Zoom (O)ut and (C)lose. You can zoom in to as few as 21 text lines, guided by the mouse pointer toward a particular area of the page if you wish. When you're zoomed in, scroll bars allow you to look around your document.

A common problem is fitting screen lines, which may be very wide, to a printed page that typically has a line length around 66 characters. If Print Preview reveals a width problem, the solution is to return to the main display and shrink the Netscape window so the lines will wrap at a shorter length.

Figure 3-10: *One of our own information pages formatted for our HP LaserJet printer.*

Close   Ctrl-W or Alt-F/C

Closes the Netscape window. If you have more than one Netscape window running (see "New Window"), that may not be the end of Netscape. You'll have to close down the other windows, natch.

Exit   Alt-F/X

This is the end of Netscape, regardless of how many Netscapes you had running.

Edit

You won't be using these features very much—in normal operations they are all grayed out, with the exceptions of Copy and Find; and even the Find feature is more conveniently invoked with the toolbar Find button.

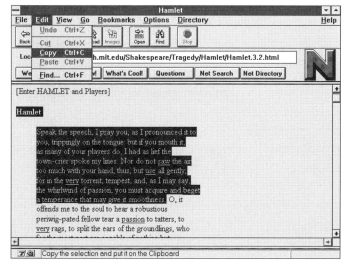

Figure 3-11: *Part of a speech from Hamlet, Act III, Scene 2, about to go on the Clipboard.*

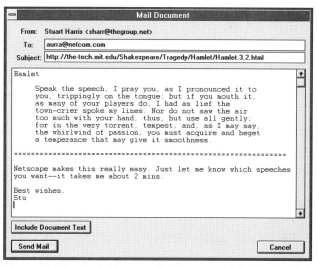

Figure 3-12: *Hamlet by e-mail. What would the Bard think of this?*

You can, however, outline any text in the Netscape content window, no matter what size or type style, and use Copy to place it on the Windows Clipboard. At any time during the same Windows session, you can drop this text fragment into any other application having Copy/Cut/Paste features: a Notepad document, for instance.

These Undo/Cut/Copy/Paste/Find edit functions really come into their own, however, when you are entering text into a WWW form or creating Netscape e-mail. See Figures 3-11 and 3-12. (The e-mail screen lacks an Edit menu, but Ctrl-V does the paste job extremely well. So does the older key combination Shift-Insert.)

View

Reload   Ctrl-R or Alt-V/R

Same as the toolbar Reload button. Remakes the same page you are currently viewing. Use if the image being loaded from cache has deteriorated.

Other Ways of Doing This
***Use the toolbar Reload button

Load Images   Ctrl-I or Alt-V/I

Used when you are running Netscape in "No in-line images" mode. Reloads the page adding the images.

Other Ways of Doing This
***Use the toolbar Images button

Refresh   Alt-V/F

This has an effect very similar to Reload, but it reloads from memory rather than from disk cache or the Web. It is intended for use during HTML editing, when you might want to reload a page without seeing the effect of a change you just made to the source document.

Source...   Alt-V/S

Well, we've mentioned the "source document" and the "source code" a few times already. This is how you see the source—it just means the page as originally coded in the HTML convention by its author. HTML enthusiasts—and that includes us—love this feature because it enables us to go to all the best-looking pages in the world and crib off their authors' work. The Web is a free-for-all that makes copyright attorneys wake up screaming in the night.

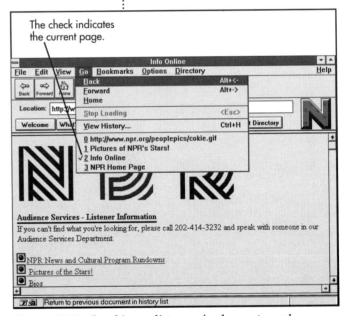

Figure 3-13: *Our history list as we've begun to explore National Public Radio's Web pages.*

Go

The Web is so endlessly fascinating that you are very likely to go wandering off across the world for hours, especially if you're using a web crawler to look up keywords. It would take a photographic memory to remember how on earth you got to where you are now. Netscape remembers for you—it keeps track of where you go and allows you to call up the history list at any time. The history list, like a trail of bread crumbs in the forest, is what enables you to retrace your steps safely. Generally these pages will be in your cache.

You can return to a previous page in your history list simply by clicking on it in the list, and it will be reloaded from the cache. You can also go back or forward one page at a time. The Go pull-down menu, as seen in Figure 3-13, is almost entirely concerned with navigating the history list in both directions.

Back   Ctrl-← or Alt-G/B

Other Ways of Doing This
***Use the toolbar Back button

Same as the Back button on the toolbar. Takes you back to the last Web page you were viewing. If you are on the first page of the session, or at the beginning of your history list, this menu option and the toolbar button are both grayed out.

Forward   Ctrl-→ or Alt-G/F

Other Ways of Doing This
***Use the toolbar Forward button

Takes you one page forward in the history list. Obviously this has no meaning unless you have already done at least one backward move.

Home   Alt-G/H

Other Ways of Doing This
***Use the toolbar Home button

Takes you immediately to your home page (as defined by you in the Preferences/Styles dialog box under Options).

Stop loading   ESC or Alt-G/S

Aborts loading of a document—usually used because loading is taking too long. Leaves you with a partially loaded page that can be viewed and used normally so far as it goes.

Other Ways of Doing This
***Use the toolbar Stop button (as long as it's showing red)

View History...   Ctrl-H or Alt-G/V

Tacked on beneath the five Go menu options is an abbreviated version of the history list itself (see Figure 3-13). You can go to any page in the list simply by clicking on that page's title in the list. For a more detailed look at the history list you can click on View History.

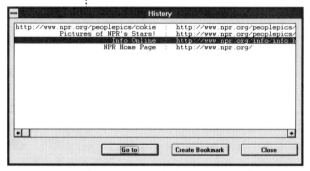

Figure 3-14: *The generous window you get when you ask for "View History."*

This nice wide window (Figure 3-14), horizontally scrollable, fits those very long URL addresses that overflow the main URL window. The most recently loaded pages are at the top. Option buttons are Go to, Create Bookmark, and Close. Double-clicking anywhere in the list reloads that page. Alt-F4 is an alternative way of closing the window, and a control button brings the normal window-sizing menu down.

Bookmarks

As you cruise the Net, you can use the Add Bookmark option to create a list of pages you might want to revisit. Once you begin to create bookmarks, a list of your bookmark pages or bookmark categories will appear here. You can go to any bookmarked page immediately by clicking on it in this list.

Creating and managing a proper hierarchy of bookmarks is a task we'll tackle in "How to Use Bookmarks" later in this chapter.

Add Bookmark   Ctrl-A or Alt-B/A

Click here to add the current page to your bookmark list. If you have already set up bookmark categories it will be added to whatever hierarchy you have specified in the Edit Bookmarks screen (the default is the top level of listings).

View Bookmarks...   Ctrl-B or Alt-B/B

Choose this option and you get an extended view of your bookmark list with editing options (see the section on "How to Use Bookmarks").

Options

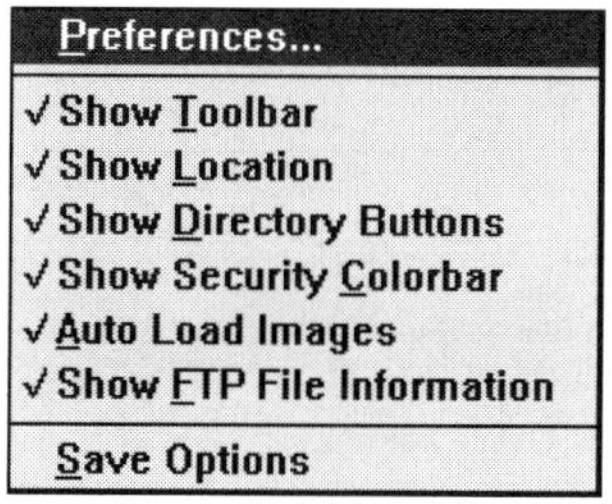

Preferences...   Alt-O/P

This menu option leads to a very extensive labyrinth of dialog boxes that set up and customize your Netscape. We covered some initial setups in Chapter 2 and will be dealing with Preferences later in this Chapter under "Setting Special Preferences."

Show Toolbar   Alt-O/T

Check to show the toolbar. Uncheck to remove the toolbar from your screen.

Show Location   Alt-O/L

If unchecked, the Location window below the toolbar which shows your current URL address goes away.

Show Directory Buttons   Alt-O/D

If unchecked, the directory buttons disappear—probably one of the first things you'll want to get rid of.

Figure 3-15: *Six toggle-check features in the Options pull-down menu.*

Show Security Colorbar

The security colorbar (see Figure 3-21) gives you information about the security of a page before you decide to transmit any information (say, a form with your credit card number in it). If you don't use this feature or don't care, you can get rid of it.

Auto Load Images   Alt-O/A

As we pointed out before, it saves lots of download time to run Netscape routinely with this option unchecked—i.e., not displaying those in-line .GIFS. However, certain Web pages make very little sense without the in-lines—and you won't be able to tell the difference between a picture and a sound bite.

Show FTP File Information   Alt-O/F

When you access anonymous FTP sites with Netscape, you get a description of contents in the available files with update notes or whatever. Uncheck this item and the file information disappears, allowing more files to be displayed on the screen.

Save Options   Alt-O/S

The way you set up your toggle checklist will be temporary, applying to this Netscape session only, unless you hit the Save Options box. Preferences are saved automatically.

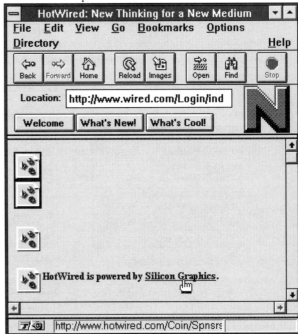

Figure 3-16: *The icon that Netscape uses to indicate a missing in-line image—and a Web page that makes no sense without the images.*

Figure 3-17: *The Directory pull-down menu.*

Directory

All but one of the options in the Directory pull-down menu take you straight to Netscape Communications Corporation where Web pages are posted to give you help and information in your explorations of the Web. (The one exception is Go to Newsgroups.) Many of these menu options duplicate functions of directory buttons. Most are self-explanatory.

Welcome!   Alt-D/W

Same as the Welcome directory button. This is the "Home Page" Netscape sets up for you by default to get you going.

What's New!   Alt-D/N

Same as the What's New! directory button This is an archived monthly update of new Internet resources—with links to the latest Web pages online.

What's Cool!   Alt-D/C

Same as the What's Cool! directory button. This is a collection of favorite Web pages by "the Supreme Arbiter of Taste" at Netscape Communications Corporation. Among the "cool stuff" is a link to The Amazing Fishcam, a "live" shot of the office fish tank (taken every minute and posted automatically). Fish lovers can note the leads to other fishy sites.

Go to Newsgroups   Alt-D/G

This is how you access USENET newsgroups. For a description of Netscape's fine Newsgroup reader, see Chapter 4 of this book.

Internet Directory   Alt-D/D

Same as the Net Directory directory button. This is a hyperlinked list of directories you can access to find things on the Internet. You can search for subjects, commercial services and business sites, and find a directory of servers here.

Internet Search   Alt-D/S

Same as the Net Search directory button. Links to various "search engines," as they're called. You can search document titles or content by WebCrawler, Lycos, etc. More on this in Chapter 6.

Internet White Pages   Alt-D/P

Trying to find someone on the Net? Use the services listed here to locate a person or organization. Several Gopher and TELNET sites collect the e-mail addresses and names of users on the Internet that can be accessed by different search means here.

About the Internet   Alt-D/A

If you're ready to study up a little further, you'll find more useful information about the Net in general here. Cocktail party experts can find excerpts from *The Whole Internet User's Guide* and *Big Dummy's Guide to the Internet* to crib from, with the lowdown on the history of the Net. Follow other links to FAQs and online guides.

Netscape Communications Corporation   Alt-D/M

Netscape Communications Corporation's home page is the place to go to find out about any new releases or the latest development in the software. You can find a current list of mirror sites here for downloading updates in the software.

Help

About Netscape...   Alt H/A

Copyright notice. (The lawyers advised them to put this page in.)

Handbook   Alt-H/A

Access to Netscape's online manual—a pretty complete reference guide to setting up and operating Netscape (though not as friendly as this book).

Release Notes   Alt-H/R

Tells you what version of Netscape you are running, with release notes concerning problems and fixes recently implemented. If you're having problems with some of your setups, you might check here.

Frequently Asked Questions   Alt H/F

Same as the Questions directory button. Besides answering basic questions, it's a useful guide to common problems users may encounter. Look here first before badgering your sysadmin.

On Security   Alt-H/F

An exhaustive explanation of how Netscape (in collaboration with RSA Data Security Inc.) handles encryption of secure pages. If that's not exhaustive enough, there are three hypertext links you can follow. We'd like to tell you where the links lead, but it's hush-hush.

How to Give Feedback   Alt-H/F

Instructions on how to tell the Netscape designers what you think of their product, and how to report bugs you think you may have found.

How to Get Support   Alt H/S

Info here is for business clients who want to use Netscape on a commercial scale and want to arrange for support services.

How to Create Web Services   Alt-D/H

If you're curious about how to create your own Web documents, go to this directory for references to documents that will tell you how to write WWW documents and direct you to HTML learning and style guides.

Directory Buttons

The directory buttons are largely a convenience for new users—useful while you're getting acquainted but quickly outgrown. Everything

Figure 3-18: *The six directory buttons*

on them is duplicated in the menu bar, either under Directory or Help. When you're ready to do away with them, uncheck Show Directory Buttons under Options, and gain a centimeter or so of page space.

Same as menu bar Directory/Welcome!

Same as menu bar Directory/What's New!

Same as menu bar Directory/What's Cool!

Same as menu bar Help/Frequently Asked Questions.

Same as menu bar Directory/Internet Search.

Same as menu bar Directory/Internet Directory.

Activity & Location Indicators

The URL Window

⟲ **HOT TIP** —

If a long and complicated URL fails, try removing everything after the basic host name plus just one slash. Then if you can get through to the host, use the URL window to add back the rest of the address, bit by bit. Or the host may offer you a link to where you want to go. It's possible the directory structure has changed or was not noted correctly.

— —

Other Ways of Doing This
***The OPEN toolbar button
(Menu File/Open Location)

Put a cursor in here with your mouse and enter a URL. Netscape will go to that address as soon as you Enter.

Note: The toolbar button is preferred if you're starting from scratch. However, this URL window is nifty if you already have an address in it. Why? To save keystrokes. There are so many URLs beginning with "http://www." that we've often wished we could macro that whole string to, let's say, Alt-H. But if you already have "http://www....bla...bla" in the window, you can use the mouse to sweep away the unwanted bla bla, then add what you need.

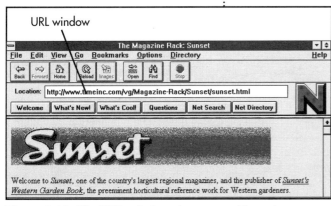

URL window

Figure 3-19: *The URL window shows you either where you are or where you're headed.*

Title Bar

The title bar is the strip at the very top between the main window buttons (Figure 3-20). You can't miss it because it's blue—or Ocean, or Hotdog-stand, or whatever took your fancy last time you were playing around with the colors on your Windows screen. When you go to a new Web page, anything that the page's author designated as "<TITLE>" in the HTML code ends up in this strip. It's usually the first part of the document to arrive, and so serves as the first indication that you've come to the right place (like the first swallow arriving at San Juan Capistrano in spring).

Some titles may be so long, or your window so narrow, that they overflow. In this case, the title is truncated from the right. URLs can become exceedingly long, and the only place you can be sure of seeing them absolutely complete is in the box you get by selecting Go/View History from the Menu bar.

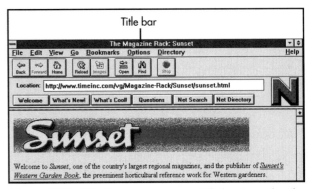

Figure 3-20: *What appears in your title bar is under the control of the page's author.*

Progress Bar

Way down at the bottom of your Netscape window is a little strip known as the progress bar. Actually, it's two separate bars, both of which inform you about progress in loading a Web page or a component such as a picture, movie or sound bite. It's certainly nice to be able to look down and see "Document Received: 22608 bytes of 107553," and then "Document Done." The thermometer bar is a comfort too, just to let you know that something's happening—but its accuracy is a bit hand-waving. It has an annoying habit of pausing just as it seems to be almost done.

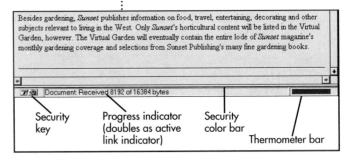

Figure 3-21: *The various components of the Netscape progress bar.*

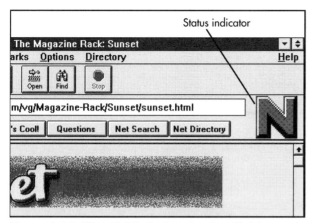

Figure 3-22: *We call this the logo but its official name is the status indicator.*

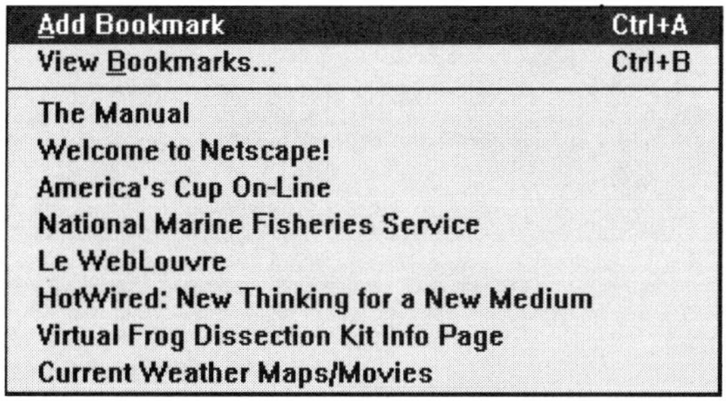

Figure 3-23: *Our first few bookmarks.*

The large progress bar also displays the URL of any active link your mouse cursor is pointing at, including the name of an external image. It can be very useful to know where you will be taken if you click on that link.

Security Indicator & Color Bars

Security was one of the principal concerns of the Internet when it was first set up as a military network in the '60s. For more than a decade now, security has taken a back seat as the Net has become a DMZ. But now, as more and more merchants are using the Web to display their wares, offering potential clients the convenience of ordering by credit card, security is once again a concern.

It is now possible to produce "secure" Web pages—meaning that the text is encrypted during transmission to you, and, even more important, that any information you enter into a form is encrypted before it leaves you. You won't find many of these yet, but when you do, Netscape will signal it for you. The narrow bars immediately above and below the page text will change from gray to blue, and the broken-key icon at the exreme lower left will change to an unbroken key on a blue background.

Status Indicator (Logo)

Animates during loading. (Actually, "pulsates" is more what it does.)

How to Use Bookmarks

Managing bookmark lists for graphical Web browsers is definitely a hang-up. The problem is that we can all imagine what our ideal bookmark manager should be like, but for an application programmer to provide the tools you need to get from here to there is quite another matter. The bookmark features of

Netscape's beta (prerelease) versions were pretty rough, and you were on your own in figuring out how to make them work. Fortunately, there has already been substantial improvement, with more undoubtedly yet to come.

It may help at the outset to realize that all of your bookmark information is contained in a file called \NETSCAPE\BOOKMARK.HTM. Take a look at it. Aha! Yes, as you make up your bookmark list you are actually creating a hypertext document.

So be patient; don't expect the computer to intuit your intentions, and before very long you'll end up with the hierarchical bookmark list of your dreams.

Creating Your First Few Bookmarks

Opinions may vary about this, but our advice is to just add your first few bookmarks in haphazard fashion by going to a page you like, and using the Menu option Bookmarks/Add Bookmark (Ctrl-A or Alt-B/A). The process happens so quickly that you won't see any evidence of your new bookmark until you click on Bookmarks in the menu bar. Then there it is, its title appended below the pull-down menu. Click on it, and you'll go right to that page.

As you add more and more of your pet pages, you'll begin to understand the need for managing the list more logically: It doesn't take too many pet pages to overflow the screen height and make that list unusable.

| Add Bookmark | Ctrl+A |
| View Bookmarks... | Ctrl+B |

The Manual
Welcome to Netscape!
America's Cup On-Line
National Marine Fisheries Service
Le WebLouvre
HotWired: New Thinking for a New Medium
WWWW - the WORLD WIDE WEB WORM
Virtual Frog Dissection Kit Info Page
ArchiePlexForm
Current Weather Maps/Movies
Welcome to the White House
SurfNet
NCAR Home Page
JumpStation Front Page
San Diego BayCam
Mark Rosenstein's Sailing Page
Laser WWW Information Server
Le Cyber-Routard
Dictionaries etc [Ref...plinary Information]
Village Schoolhouse
Exploratorium Home Page
The Magazine Rack: Sunset

Figure 3-24: *At about this point, we knew our bookmark list needed organizing.*

Categorizing Bookmark Lists

The first step is to move your bookmarks around so that they are grouped in categories. Think about the categories that would be useful to you personally. In the list shown in Figure 3-24, some obvious

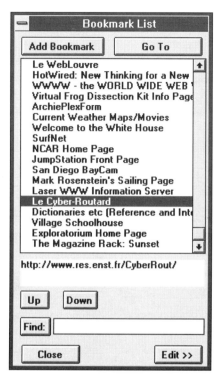

Figure 3-25: *The "elementary" side of the bookmark window.*

categories would be Reference, Educational and Magazines. The rest can be grouped as General for now.

The bookmark editing window comes in two parts, which might be thought of as elementary and advanced. Get the elementary window up using Menu Bookmarks/View Bookmarks (Ctrl-B or Alt-B/B).

Now you can use the mouse to highlight any bookmark in the list, making it the "current" bookmark. A double-click, or a click on the Go To button sends Netscape off to that particular bookmarked page. Notice that the Up/Dn/PgUp/PgDn/Home/End keys on your keyboard, as well as the scroll bars, navigate the list. Next, get used to the idea that you can move the current bookmark around the list using the Up and Down buttons. It's dead easy: pretty soon you'll have all your bookmarks grouped.

Adding Headers & Separators

What we're working toward is having a pull-down bookmark menu that includes Reference, Educational, Magazines, and whatever else we choose, so that highlighting Magazines produces the Magazine list to pick from, and so on. That's what is meant by a hierarchical list—and we're not there yet.

To get there, you need to graduate to the "advanced" window. Do this by clicking on the Edit >> button at the extreme lower right.

Now as you cruise your list, you can see some of the extra information that Netscape stores for you on each item in the list: its URL address, obviously, but also the date/time you created it and last visited it. There's also a generous-sized window in which you can write a mini-essay singing the praises of this page. Note that although this window does not have Edit Cut/Copy/Paste options of its own, anything on the edit Clipboard (such as text you outlined in the page itself) can be dropped into this space using Ctrl-V.

By far the most interesting button is the one labeled "New Header." When you use it, the header will pop in immediately below the current list item. So position the list selector just above one of your category groupings, press New Header and enter the category label in the Name: window. Your header now appears in the main list, with a hyphen at the extreme left identifying it visually.

Now it's a matter of telling Netscape which items on your bookmark list belong to that category. And here the Netscape coders have elected to make this an extra function of the Up and Down buttons rather than a separate function. Here's how it works:

Items that belong to a header are indented under that header. You'll find that an item will move up the list using the Up button, but when you push it up against a Header or an indented item, it indents instead of moving. (Conversely, moving an indented item with the Down button cancels indentation when it hits a non-indented line.) So, in Figure 3-26, moving Virtual Frog Dissection Kit "Up" will indent it and make it belong to the Educational category. Start with the first item under each header, then click on "Up" and it will indent. Move down to the next item and repeat until all the items under the header are indented.

Repeat that process for all your categories. Then use the "New Separator" button to add a line between categories and make the list even clearer. It finishes off the list like you see in Figure 3-27 and has the desired result on your main screen's pull-down menus as shown in Figure 3-28.

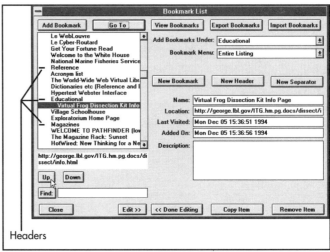

Figure 3-26: *A click on the Up button indents the Virtual Frog, making it part of the "Educational" bookmark list.*

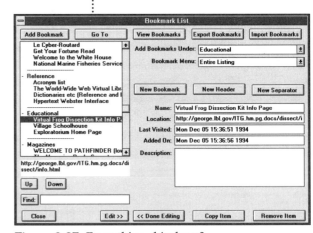

Figure 3-27: *Everything shipshape?*

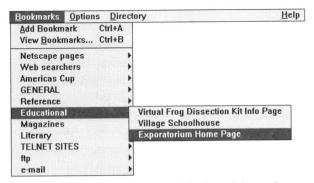

Figure 3-28: *A truly hierarchical bookmark list at last.*

Going back to the bookmark edit screen, you'll discover that if you make a Header the current item, pressing the Up or Down button moves the Header together with its entire indented sublist. Also, pressing Remove Item, which would normally just delete a redundant bookmark, now deletes the whole sublist. (Netscape has the grace to warn you and ask for confirmation before going ahead.)

Now, if you feel like getting really clever some rainy day, prove to yourself that you can set up second-level headers (double-indented), then third-, fourth-, fifth-level headers to make a superlist. One possible use for this would be to keep personal lists for several people sharing a computer: The top-level headers might be TOM, ROBERTA, AHMED, and the next level could be Tom's Art List and Ahmed's Business Sites. A level below might be a division between USA/Europe, and so on.

HOT TIP

If you have a particularly complex bookmark list, make a backup copy of the file BOOKMARK.HTM. Otherwise, a disk crash could wipe out all of your list-management work.

Other Bookmark Options

Now that you have a decently ordered list, you can make use of a couple of other Netscape bookmark-management features.

Use the Bookmark Menu pop-up to tell Netscape to show you only one of your categories as opposed to the Entire Listing (which means just your top-level Headers). Use Add Bookmarks Under to tell Netscape that until further notice any bookmarks you add belong in the Reference category (or whatever).

If your bookmark list gets very complicated and you'd like to see a simplified version of it in the bookmark edit window, you can make all bookmarks that belong under a header disappear by double-clicking on the header. A plus sign (+) will appear to the left of the header to remind you of the unseen bookmarks, and they can be brought back anytime you like by double-clicking on the same header again.

Turning Your Bookmark List Into a Web Page

Don't forget, your bookmark list is actually a hypertext document. To prove it, use the View Bookmarks button, then close this window (Escape will do as well as the Close button) and behold your list looking just like a Web page! You can use it as you would any Web page, following the hypertext links to your bookmarked pages. For this title, it uses the name you provided under Mail in the Preferences/Mail and Proxies box.

Exporting & Importing Bookmarks

These options simply allow you to save the list under any name (Export) or implement a bookmark file created by another application using Netscape's indent rules (Import). Obviously, these options also offer a way of managing several alternative bookmark lists (like a "weekend" list with sports and restaurant pages).

Making Your Bookmark List Your Home Page

Since your bookmark list is an actual Web document, it's possible to make that your home page and make accessing your favorite pages easy. Doing so is slightly tricky, however. This is how:

Go to the Options menu, choose Preferences then the Styles dialog box. In the default home page window, enter this:

file:///C:1/PATH/FILE.HTM

(where FILE.HTM is the name of your bookmark file. It could be your BOOKMARK.HTM or something else you've saved it under). The entry is case-sensitive, so enter it exactly.

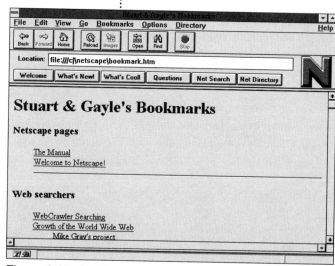

Figure 3-29: *Our bookmark list turned into a personal Web page.*

HOT TIP —·—·—·—·—·—·—·—·—·—·—·—

After any extensive editing work, always press the Done Editing button before closing this window. Otherwise, certain edits may not be saved properly.

—·—·—·—·—·—·—·—·—·—·—·—·—

Setting Special Preferences

No doubt once you get familiar with Netscape you'll want to customize it for your own use, perhaps configuring the screen to look the way you want or adding new helper applications you collect on your Web cruises. Some Preferences you have already set just to get Netscape running properly. Other settings are at the tip of your mouse finger whenever you want them.

Choose Preferences under the Options pull-down menu. The pop-up menu at the head of the Preferences dialog box lets you determine whether the box is going to be concerned with Styles (screen appearance); Directories, Applications and News; Network, Images and Security; Mail and Proxies; or Helper Applications.

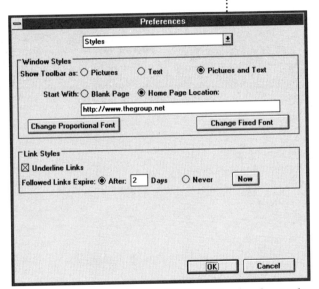

Figure 3-30: *The Preferences/Styles dialog box has to do with the look of your Netscape screen.*

Styles

Radio buttons allow you to select the appearance of the toolbar, and an input window is available for you to set the URL of your home page. This is important: the default is the Netscape Welcome page, and after you've seen that little green monster pop up a few times, you'll want to select something else. Once you've got your bookmarks all nicely organized, you might want to make your BOOKMARK.HTM file your default home page. (See the sidebar in the previous section.)

Buttons are provided for selecting from a range of fonts for the general text on your page; and a check box lets you decide whether you want links underlined.

Links are the hypertext words that appear in blue and (by default) underlined on your screen, letting you know that a different page can be accessed by clicking on the appropriate word(s). Once you have visited a page, its link changes color from blue to purple—a nice feature that shows you at a glance which of the links you have already followed.

To say that the Web changes frequently is the understatement of the year—so it makes little sense for your followed links to be in a different color forever. The remaining buttons on the Styles box let you say how soon you want this feature to "expire," meaning revert to the same color as links you have never followed. One option is Now, another is Never, and you can specify any number of days in between.

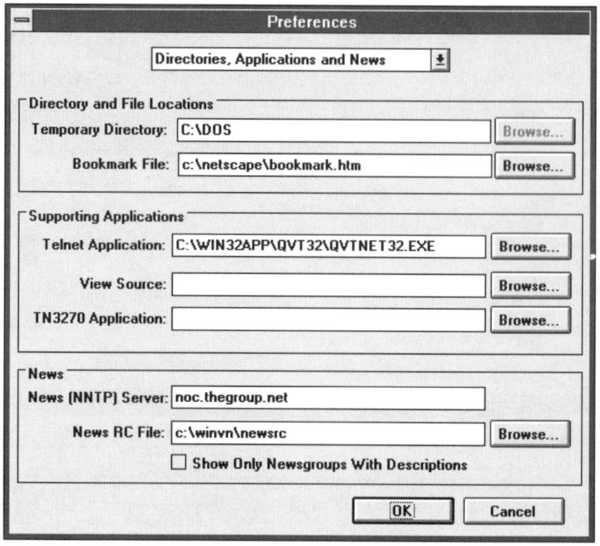

Figure 3-31: *A few things that Netscape has to be told about.*

Directories, Applications & News

The Directory and File Location boxes allow you to change the default location of the BOOKMARK.HTM file and the temporary files. Temporary files are created by Netscape whenever it is about to use a helper application to display something. After shuttling the helper application and its data file in and out of memory, the temporary file is automatically deleted.

The Supporting Applications box is where you enter the location and name of helper applications for TELNET and TN3270 sessions (see Chapter 4), also any application you'd like to use to display (and possibly also edit, save, etc.) source code files. If you leave this box blank, source files will be displayed in Netscape's built-in window, which has no edit or save features.

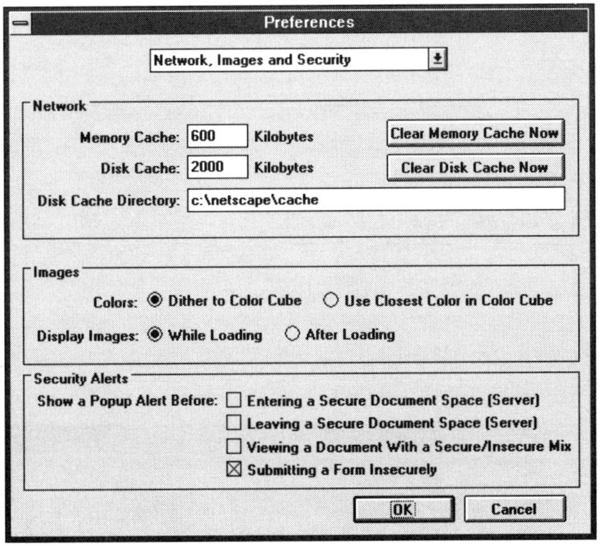

Figure 3-32: *Here's where you manage your cache, your color and your security alerts.*

The News box down at the bottom has to do with Netscape's USENET News service, and you have to pay some attention to this or you won't be getting any news. First, you must fill in the Internet address of your news server. This is the computer that your system uses to gather USENET news files. All newsreaders need to be told this, and if you don't know it, ask your sysadmin.

The NEWSRC file is the data file that keeps track of the newsgroups you are subscribed to and the articles you have already read. It's perfectly safe to allow this to default to C:\NETSCAPE\NEWSRC. However, if you already use a newsreader, you may have the option of telling Netscape to use an existing NEWSRC file—one that you have created for the WINVN newsreader, for instance. Simply enter the directory path, and all the subscription and catch-up information in NEWSRC will automatically appear in Netscape.

ⓞ HOT TIP

Trumpet News—one of the very best newsreaders—has a somewhat different format for its subscription record file.

Network, Images & Security

Here's where you can specify how much memory and disk space you want to make available for the cache, according to the size of your system. The disk cache fills up very quickly and does not clear when you end your Netscape session. You can clear it with the Clear Disk Cache Now button. You might also use this when you have reason to suspect that a page is loading from cache rather than the online source, and therefore showing you a version that's out of date.

Other options in this dialog box include specifying whether you want to see images forming while they're downloading and whether you want to be advised of security features when they are available on a Web page.

HOT TIP

If you don't care about security and hate to be reminded every time you're doing something with security implications, uncheck all the check boxes in the Security Alerts subbox.

Mail & Proxies

Just as Netscape needs to know the address of your News server if it's to serve you with News, it needs to know about your mail server so that you can use it to send e-mail. It's possible that your News server and your Mail server are the same machine, but not very likely. Again, if you don't know, ask your sysadmin. Filling in your name and e-mail address is also well worthwhile—for the keystrokes it will save when it's time to mail something.

If your Internet connection is through a large company or institution it's possible that you're working behind what's called a fire wall—a device used to ensure the security against outside hackers. If this is the case, you'll need to make use of something called a "proxy" to make your Internet connection. Ask your systems administrator what you need to put here to make your connections.

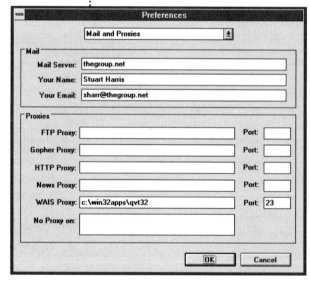

Figure 3-33: *In this dialog box, you need to tell Netscape about your mail server.*

Helper Applications

Netscape (unlike Mosaic) has its own built-in viewer that displays images in .GIF, .JPEG and .XBM format. However, the viewer is not as versatile as a dedicated image-viewer like LVIEW. And Netscape has (so far) no built-in application to run movies, hear audio, or deal with many, many file types you may find yourself bringing to your computer with Netscape's help.

This screen displays and manages a list of all these file types. By default it lists 4 types of video, 3 types of text, 11 possible picture formats, 3 audio formats and 11 application types. If that menu is not comprehensive enough for you, you can add more of these so-called "Mime types" by pressing that New button and entering the details in a dialog box.

Your task is to go through this list, clicking on every file type that you think you will ever be interested in downloading from the Net, and telling Netscape how you want to handle it. Until you make the decision, a row of question marks (?????) appears in the "Action" column of the Mime-type box.

Your choices are:

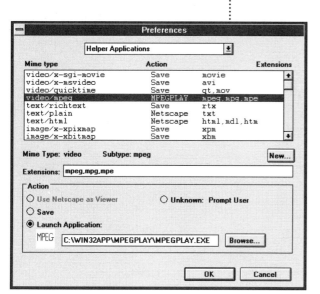

Figure 3-34: *An example of how to tell Netscape you want movies of .MPEG format to be played by MPEGPLAY.*

1. Let Netscape's own software display it—only available for a minority of Mime types.

2. Defer a decision by declaring "Unknown: Prompt User" (that's you).

3. Immediately save it to a local file, leaving the display decision for later. (This is what you will want to do with .EXE and .ZIP files, to name but two.)

4. Define a helper application—i.e., a whole different piece of software—that will handle this type of file. You may well want movies with file extensions .MPG, .MPEG, .MPE to be sent straight to your MPEGPLAY.EXE for viewing. Here's how:

Click on the "video/mpeg" line in the Mime-type window. See it become highlighted and the fields underneath fill in as:

Mime Type: video   Subtype: mpeg   Extensions: mpg, mpeg, mpe (You may edit the extensions field.)

Now bring the mouse cursor into the lower box and click on the Launch Application radio button. If you know the exact path to MPEGPLAY, you can enter it manually in the application window—but you'll probably prefer to click on the Browse button and go find it by "hunt-and-click." Figure 3-34 shows the complete box.

HOT TIP

It's worth making a thorough job of these helper applications. If you leave out some file types that you later need to handle in special ways, you'll probably have forgotten how to do all this. Having done it, make a backup copy of your NETSCAPE.INI file, where all those decisions you just made are enshrined.

Moving On

If you're like most people, you will continue to discover new features of Netscape as you use it. By now, besides learning how to navigate around the Web with Netscape, you should have learned how to do the following:

- Change the look of your screen to suit you, including gaining maximum screen space when you want it.
- Handle files you want to save, send to someone or manipulate.
- Set up your bookmarks list and manage it as it grows.
- Set up helper applications for video and audio and make changes in the future.

In the next chapter we'll go into some of the special features you'll want to use, including using Netscape to do FTP, search the Net and access newsgroups. We'll also look at some of the types of pages you can find on the Web to give you some starting points for exploration.

LAUNCHING INTO CYBERSPACE

Being inveterate travelers, the first thing we do when we arrive in a strange city is take off on a walking tour. We're usually too anxious to have a look around to bother with a map, and we've had plenty of time to peruse the travel guides at home.

You've probably felt the same way about this new cybercommunity you've just discovered. Unless you're an extremely methodical person, you probably didn't wait to get all of your helper applications installed before you took off on your first walk around the Web neighborhood.

So, in this chapter we'll take a closer look at things like movie and audio files and in-line images and the helper applications you need to run them. You'll find out how to download hypermedia files and save them for off-line replay, and how to copy images you might want to use in your own documents. We'll show you the kinds of Web pages that are available online, to give you a starting point for your own explorations.

Then we'll talk about those all-important Internet features like FTP, TELNET, Gopher and USENET that are all made available to you in a new easy format with Netscape's interface. And finally we'll tell you how to keep abreast of program updates and point you to some information sites and newsgroups that will help you sort out problems and find solutions.

Hypermedia in Netscape

If you're to get the best out of the Web experience, you need to understand how hypermedia is presented to you—that way you'll appreciate better what is and isn't possible. A good example is the difference between an "in-line" and an "external" image.

It's much *less* important to understand the difference between .GIF, .JPEG and the other half dozen or so image formats—so let's get that out of the way quickly.

Still Photos: .GIFs & .JPEGs

Those alphabet soup file extensions all refer to different ways of encoding a picture for storage as an ordinary computer data file. The granddaddy of them all is .TIFF —the Tagged Image File Format, which creates humongous files. Many other formats, including the very popular .GIF (Graphics Interchange Format), were invented in an attempt to compress the data more effectively. A few years ago, an expert committee called the Joint Photographic Experts Group thrashed out a new format which was supposed to supplant all others and become an industry standard. Hence, the .JPEG (or .JPG) format, which has so far failed to become the standard—but it may nevertheless be the best.

Still Photos: In-Lines & Externals

For a not-very-complex color picture, it's generally true to say .GIF is the most compact format but .JPEG offers better quality in the end.

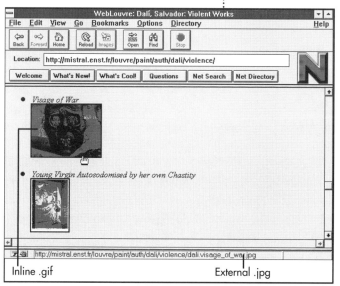

Figure 4-1: *The small in-line image of Dali's "Visage of War" is a .GIF , but the actual image we are about to download is a .JPEG, with much finer detail.*

Hence, .GIF is the format invariably used to create all the little "thumbnail" images that decorate Web pages. Data compression, in this case, is more important than quality. Because they are really considered part of the document (even though you can choose not to see them by unchecking Auto Load Images in the Options pull-down menu), they're known as in-line images. In our own Web page design we are careful not to be carried away using these, simply because they can slow down page-loading so much.

An external image is not part of the document you load, but it is referenced by a *link*—either hypertext, like an underlined word, or another type of link. It's these external images that are frequently in .JPEG format, because load time can (within reason) be sacrificed for quality. Where it gets confusing is when an in-line .GIF is used as the link to an external .JPEG. It's actually a very common technique—used in the Dali exhibit of the "WebLouvre" depicted in Figure 4-1. Perhaps now you can better understand why this is often done.

When you download an external image in .GIF , .JPEG or .XBM format, you can use Netscape's own built-in viewer to see it right there in the content window (here's where you may want to enlarge your window by unchecking the Show Toolbar, Location and Directory Buttons in the Options pull-down menu). For any other image format, you will need a "helper application" in the form of a viewer.

Actually, we recommend that you get and install the helper called LVIEW, and use it for images you especially prize even if they're in .JPEG format. For one thing, LVIEW lets you manipulate the image in ways Netscape's own viewer doesn't even attempt. For another, in dealing with external images you have only the View or Save option. There is no option to View Then Save. This means that you may have spent a little time finding that Dali picture and then only view it fleetingly rather than adding it to a collection.

Switch between View And Save in the Preferences/Helper Applications dialog box—see Chapter 3. LVIEW is available at

ftp://gatekeeper.dec.com/pub/micro/msdos/win3/desktop

The file is lview31.zip.

QuickTime & MPEG Movies

On-Web movies, fortunately, do not come in such a bewildering variety of formats and flavors. Most of them, perhaps 99 percent of them, either are in the "Macintosh" standard known as QuickTime, or are the product of another expert committee, the Motion Picture Experts Group—guess what? An .MPEG, of course.

Netscape has no built-in movie viewer, and you really need helpers for both .MPEG and QuickTime formats, since they are about equally common, and the allegiance of Mac and Windows to the two rival formats is now pretty much irrelevant. The eventual image quality is about the same, but QuickTime is a better bet if you want to try for sound in sync. Until this technology moves on a bit, don't expect movie-theater quality. We recommend that you set your helper application preference to "save" rather than "launch the helper" because down-

Where to Get Your Movie Viewers MPEGPLAY is available at

ftp://gatekeeper.dec.com/pub/micro/msdos/win3/desktop

The files are:
mpegw11d.zip for Windows 3.1
mpegw32g.zip for Windows NT/Windows 95

A QuickTime viewer is at Imperial College, London:

ftp://lister.cc.ic.ac.uk/pub/wingopher/viewers/movies

The file is:**qtwplay.zip**

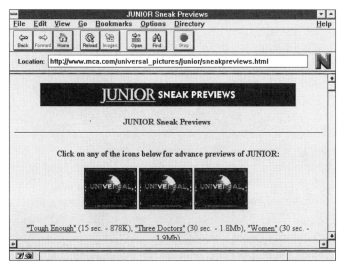

Figure 4-2: *Take advantage of Universal's new sneak previews.*

Figure 4-3: *The little icon you will often see as a link to an audio file.*

loading a movie file takes a while, and if there's a last-minute accident at least you won't have to go through that again.

If you're equipped with movie helpers, you can enjoy Web services like Universal's new sneak previews (Figure 4-2). Better have plenty of disk space: these short clips are around 2mb each!

Audio

The surprising thing about Web audio files, at least to those of us who are nonexperts, is that they are as huge as or huger than video files. It's not uncommon to find a sound bite lasting just 30 seconds taking up several megabytes of disk space.

A really well-behaved Web page (like the ones we design, natch) tells you how big an audio or video file is, so you can decide whether you have that much time to spend downloading it. Unfortunately, many HTML authors get too carried away by their artistic page makeup to worry about "technical details" like that (or are working on university supercomputers and don't think about those of us on little PCs), and the information is not available. Netscape helps things along, actually—it will generally give you progress information at the lower left corner of the screen. So if you're already running late for an appointment and you see "Document Received 821 of 4566307 Bytes" down there, that's when you click on Stop to bail out.

The icon shown in Figure 4-3 is actually from a "First Family" page from The White House (**http://www.whitehouse.gov**), and it's nice of them to tell us that the sound of Socks mewing is a 36k file. They might have added that it's in .AU format, to be *really* kind.

Our advice is the same as for movie files: Set your Preferences/Helper Applications to save rather than launch your application immediately. We'll add more advice, too: Don't let these things accumulate on your disk—they're just too big to give house-room to unless you have good reason.

Audio files come in two different formats, but it's no problem—the best audio player is called WPLANY, short for "We Play Anything." Find it at

ftp://ftp.cam.org/systems/ms-windows/slip-ppp/ VIEWERS

The file is: **wplny09b.zip**

Another audio player—highly sophisticated—is WHAM, to be found at the **gatekeeper.dec** site under the name **wham131.zip**. (See the sidebar, page 66.)

Of course, to hear any of these wild and wonderful sounds you need a sound card and a pair of loud-speakers... Or do you?

Forms

There are many times when it's appropriate for the flow of information from the Web to you to be put in reverse: when you need to put information in rather than pull it out. One simple case in point is searching for keywords—how's a web crawler to know what *you* want to know if you can't tell it?

Another good example is a feedback page, on which somebody invites you to enter some informa-tion. Netscape invites your feedback in a page you'll find under "How to Give Feedback" in the Main menu's Help pull-down. Another example is shown in Figure 4-5. All

Sound Power

Here's how to make your tinny little PC loud-speaker work for a living. If you can't afford a sound blaster (or don't want to make your system *too* attractive to the kids), you can divert audio to your built-in PC speaker—the one that thought it was going to spend its entire life saying nothing more elaborate than "BEEP." Follow these steps:

1. Grab **WPLANY.EXE** from the FTP site above, and install it.

2. Go to the Preferences/Helper Applications dialog box and instruct Netscape to launch WPLANY whenever you download .WAV, .AU. or .SND. files.

3 Grab a file called **SPEAK.EXE** from **ftp://ftp.microsoft.com/Softlib/MSLFILES**

Put SPEAK.EXE in its own subdirectory and run it under DOS. It will self-extract, producing the files **SPEAKER.DRV** and **OEMSETUP.INF.**

4. Fire up Windows, and activate the Control Panel utility (in the Main program group).

5. Click on Drivers, then select the Add button. Select Unlisted Or Updated Driver from the list. Enter the path to the **OEMSETUP.INF** you just created (that's what Windows is looking for). →

6. If all is well, "Sound Driver for PC-Speaker" will pop up as the single item on a list. Select OK. You'll hear other-worldly sounds as your little speaker wakes up and says "Oh wow! I get to do something more important than BEEP????"

7. Choose Restart Windows.

8. Now you'll hear things whenever you end a Windows session or select an illegal option. If this does not please you, bring back the Control Panel, click on Sounds, and uncheck the Enable System Sounds box.

9. Any audio you grab from the net is going to sound really terrible. Quit being so stingy—go out and buy a Sound Blaster. The computer hardware industry needs your money!!!

such page features are known collectively as "forms," and they seem to get more complex and more ingenious all the time.

Undoubtedly, one of the driving forces behind the development of forms is Web commerce. Figure 4-5 shows an order form (for fresh flowers, in this case) complete with credit card information.

Exploring Cyberspace

The day when dry tomes from the catacombs of science and esoteric discussions of quarks dominated the Web is fast disappearing. There are still tons of good references for real and would-be scientists on the Web—in fact, they form a strong backbone to the system. But the diversity of resources devoted to the wide range of human interests is expanding daily on the Web.

Among the types of Web sites you can visit now are electronic newspapers and magazines, museums and art galleries, entertainment resources, business and commercial outlets, along with many sites run by government, academic or private institutions sharing their own special databases and information.

To give you a feel for the diversity of the Web we've collected some outstanding sites in various categories. We've even made it easy for you by including them in our *Netscape Quick Tour Online Companion.* Go to **http://www.vmedia.com/** and you'll find hypertext links to other Web resources. Take them as starting points and then wander at will. To quote Dr. Seuss, "Oh, the places you'll go!"

Electronic Publications

Time-Life Publishing

Here you can find an online edition of *Time* magazine with excerpts from the latest issue, as well as excerpts from several other Time-Life-owned magazines, such as *Southern Living*, *Sunset* and *Entertainment Weekly*. You can choose a low-speed (fewer graphics) or high-speed (more goodies) version to suit your taste and computer capacity. *Entertainment Weekly*'s capsule movie reviews are a particularly nice resource.
http://www.timeinc.com/pathfinder/

Hotwired

"Hotwired" is the online version of *Wired* magazine, where all the techno-hip cognoscenti hang out. The graphics on its online edition are really exceptional, and the publication is state-of-the-art in Web publishing.
http://www/wired.com

Some other magazines to peruse:
Boardwatch: **http://www.boardwatch.com**
Mother Jones: **http://www.mojones.com/**
motherjones.html
VIBE: **http://www.timeinc.com/vibe/**
VibeOnline!.html
Washington Weekly: **http://dolphin.gulf.net**
PC Week and *PC Magazine:* **http://www.ziff.com**

News & Sports

A whole host of newspapers are jumping into the online publishing arena. One of the best lists of online

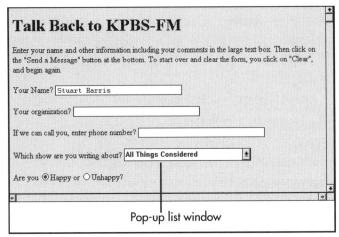

Figure 4-4: *In this local radio feedback page designed by Mark Burgess, "All Things Considered" was selected from a pop-up list of all NPR's regular programs.*

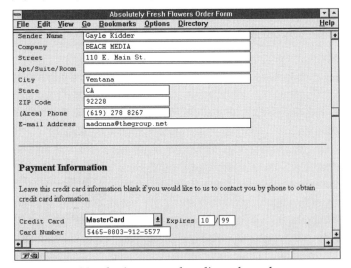

Figure 4-5: *No, that's not a real credit card number—are you kidding?*

newspapers is maintained at
http://www.nando.net/epage/htdocs/links/newspapers.html

Among the news sources with links to this page are *USA Today*, the *San Francisco Chronicle & Examiner, Boston Globe*, "CNN Headline News" and the (London) *Times* literary supplement.

For international news links, go to
http://www.cs.vu.nl/~gerben/news.html

Sports news and the latest scores in football, basketball, baseball, hockey and soccer are a popular resource at
http://www.cfn.cs.dal.ca/Media/TodaysNews/SportStuff.html

More football scores at
http://www.nando.net/football/1994/fbserv.html

The latest tennis results can be found at
http://arganet.tenagra.com/Racquet_Workshop/Workshop.html

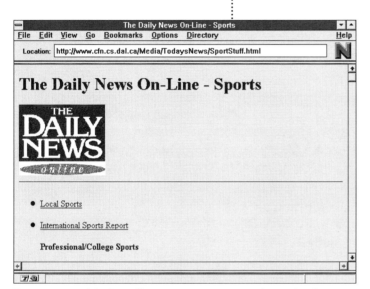

Figure 4-6: *This Canadian page is a great starting point for sports fans.*

Museums & Art Galleries

Le WebLouvre

This is the model that many other museums are trying to follow as they go online. See highlights of exhibits at the Louvre in Paris and as an added attraction, take a "walking tour" of Paris. Nobody knows a good tourist lure like the Parisians.
http://www.mistral.enst.fr/louvre/

There's a mirror site at **http://sunsite.unc.edu/louvre**

The Smithsonian

Visit the Smithsonian Institution in Washington, D.C., and you'll find a wealth of resources for teachers, students and the aimlessly curious. These pages are still in development, but you can access the National Museum of Natural History, the National Air & Space Museum and the Smithsonian Education Server, among other pages.
http://www.si.edu

The Exploratorium

The online interface of this many-faceted museum in the Palace of Fine Arts in San Francisco is a labyrinth for exploring science and nature topics.
http://www.exploratorium.edu

Scripps Institution of Oceanography

The aquarium-museum at this landmark oceanographic institution on the Pacific shores in San Diego has information on marine animals, tidepools, and current research on the oceans and atmosphere.
http://aqua.ucsd.edu

Educational Resources

The Village Schoolhouse

Dozens of resources for teachers, students and home-schoolers. New projects being added constantly. Teachers can visit the K-12 Teacher's Lounge and exchange projects and information.
http://crusher.bev.net:80/education/index.html

Curry School

The Curry School at the University of Virginia is dedicated to encouraging interactive education with computers for kids. This is another

rich source of educational materials for elementary and high school teachers and students.
http://curry.edschool.virginia.edu

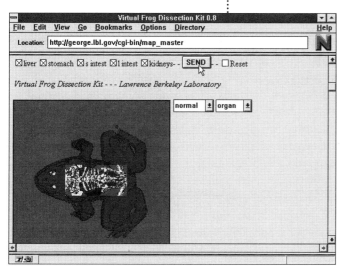

Figure 4-7: *The World Wide Web must have saved the lives of a few thousand frogs already.*

Sea World/Busch Gardens

Sea World maintains a great animal database, useful for teachers and students.
http://crusher.bev.net:80/education/SeaWorld

Virtual Frogs

It had to happen: dissecting cyberfrogs . Two sites have actually come up with their demo projects for school use, one run by Lawrence Berkeley Laboratories (Figure 4-7), the other by Curry School at the University of Virginia. Try your lab skills at
http://george.lbl.gov/ITG.hm.pg.docs/dissect/info.html
http://curry.edschool.virginia.edu/~insttech/frog

American Memory Project

The Library of Congress sponsors this Web site in progress, which contains a collection of primary source and archival material on American culture and history. Includes historical photographs from the Civil War to the present, speeches by American leaders during and after World War I and lots of photos and bibliographical material.
http://lcweb2.loc.gov/amhome.html

Government & Institutions

U.S. Government Master Page

This is the central address for government information pages. From here, you can split off to your favorite branch—Executive, Legislative

or Judicial (remember your civics class?), plus a number of government-related independent agencies like the Small Business Administration. You can even get your tax forms by e-mail.
http://www.alw.nih.gov/govt.html

The White House
If it's the Prez you're interested in, you can skip the previous page and go straight to the White House. Take a tour of the interior or see The Man himself at play with the family cat—who looks like she'd rather be in Arkansas.
http://www.whitehouse.gov

NASA
Seems every net jockey in the world is interested in rockets and spaceships. NASA's home pages are among the most visited on the Web. Here you can get the latest news on space shuttle missions and view some of the wealth of space imagery generated by NASA's activities.
http://hypatia.gsfc.nasa.gov/NASA_homepage.html

Business & Commercial

Open Market Inc.
Visit the Open Market for a directory of commercial services, products and information on the Internet. See What's New or search for a product on the net. Our search for "flowers" turned up 13 online florists.
http://www.directory.net

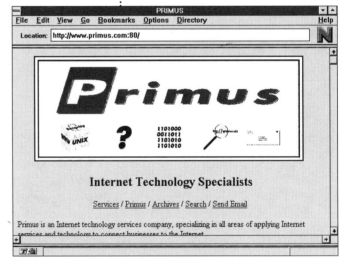

Figure 4-8: *So much business is being done on the Web these days that Web business is a business itself.*

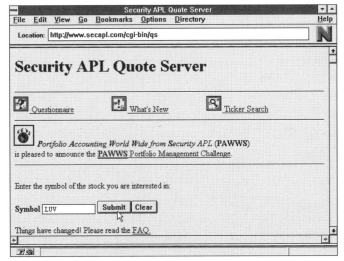

Figure 4-9: *This investment service offers a full range of business information, plus free stock quotes.*

Interesting Business Sites

The businesses in this list are personally selected by Bob O'Keefe at the School of Management, Rensselaer Polytechnic Institute, and updated monthly. He keeps a keen eye out for the latest business developments on the net.
http://www.rpi.edu/~okeefe/business.html

Internet Business Center

This is a great resource for business activities on the Web—including statistics on the latest commercial sites and traffic.
http://tig.com/IBC/index.html

Stock Market Updates

Several services offer stock quotes and market rates online. For a fee, a number of them allow you to register your portfolio to receive closing prices every day. We like the site run by Security APL Inc., which as a come-on to their services lets you get free quotes, one at a time. Their Market Watch Page is updated every three minutes during trading hours. Access at
http://www.secapl.com

Databases

U.S. Census Information Server

The Census Bureau posts population statistics; financial data on state and local governments and schools; county and city data; and census bureau publications.
http://www.census.gov/

The Human Genome Project

The Human Genome Project has taken on the monumental task of mapping every chromosome and writing down the complete genetic code that describes a human being, letter by letter. Scientists and medical specialists around the world access this database, which is constantly updated. A fascinating peek into the invisible parameters of our humanity. **http://www.hgmp.mrc.ac.uk/HUMAN-GEN-DB.html**

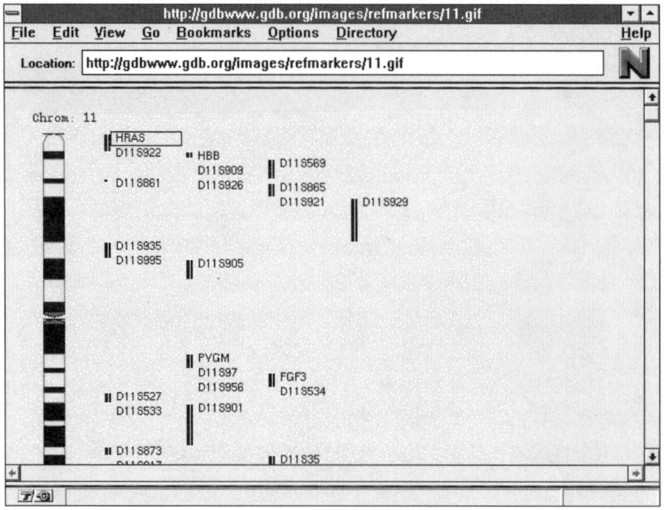

Movies & Entertainment

Cardiff Movie Database Browser

Pages for film buffs and trivia quiz masters. Search for movie titles, actors, directors, what have you. **http://www.cm.cf.ac.uk/Movies/**

Movie Studios

Visit the movie studios and see previews of coming attractions in downloadable QuickTime clips. You can even visit the Press Room.

Buena Vista Pictures:
http://bvp.wdp.com:80/index.html

Universal Pictures:
http://www.mca.com/

Figure 4-10: *Genetic databases, like this chromosome map, could hardly be better suited to the Internet.*

Travel

The London Guide

This is one of our favorite places to visit when one of us (guess which one) gets homesick. Designed by University College, London, these pages are a resource for Londoners and tourists alike, with guides to the theater scene, pubs, restaurants, hotels, and even a "Tube Journey Planner" that plots your route on the London Underground.
http://www.web.cs.ucl.ac.uk/misc/uk/london.html

The Big Island of Hawaii

Blizzard outside? Think you'll never see the sun again? Take a break and visit Hawaii. Meet the people, tour the countryside and visit the volcanos at this smartly produced site from the Irvine bookstore with excerpts from the Moon Travel Handbook on Hawaii.
http://bookweb.cwis.uci.edu:8042/Books/Moon/Hawaii.html

Personal Home Pages

The World Wide Web Virtual Library
Home Page Directory

One of the best ways to discover interesting Web sites is to find out where other Web users are spending their time. If it's cool or interesting, you can bet other people have put it on their private lists. This repository of selected home pages includes those devoted to special interests as well as general resources.
http://web.city.ac.uk/citylive/pages.html

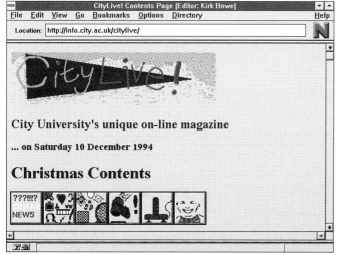

Figure 4-11: *This University page provides, among other goodies, an index of home pages.*

Internet Services via Netscape

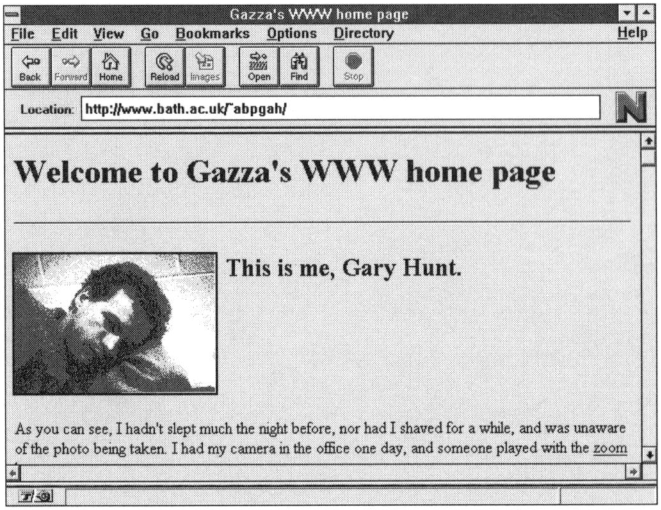

After a few weeks cruising the Web, you get so used to seeing "http://" up there in the URL window that you might start thinking of the entire Internet world in terms of http addresses. In fact, http (HyperText Transport Protocol) is the data-exchange protocol that made the Web possible, but it's far from being the only allowable prefix to URL addresses. Actually, it merely specifies a type of server—the one whose exact address makes up the next part of the URL.

Almost all the "traditional" Internet protocols have server addresses that are accessible by Netscape. It's perfectly legitimate to construct a URL beginning **gopher://, ftp://, or telnet://**—and by a kind of trickery, the prefix mailto: brings e-mail transmission to your Netscape screen. Even Finger (get login information) and Archie (search FTP sites for keywords) services are available, thanks to so-called "gateways" made available by some major Web servers and accessed as http addresses.

Figure 4-12: *Home page of Gary "Gazza" Hunt—a friend we "met on the net."*

E-Mail

Netscape, as already mentioned, has a fine outgoing mail service accessed from the Main menu File/Mail Document (or Ctrl-M). It can convey an ordinary e-mail message, or you can include a complete or partial text of the current page or anything on the Windows Clipboard. If you are trying to use this service and getting constant errors, it's likely to be because you have not set your Preferences-Mail dialog correctly to point Netscape at your mail server machine.

So if you want to send a message to **juliaZ@almond.ulua.edu**, the obvious way is to press Ctrl-M, enter Julia's address, change the subject header if need be (it defaults to the URL of the current page), make your message and send it. But another way is to turn Julia's address into a pseudo-URL, using the prefix "mailto:" Select the toolbar Open button and enter **mailto:juliaZ@almond.ulua.edu** in the URL window. You'll find it brings up the e-mail form with the address already filled out and a blank subject header.

So what's the big deal? The big deal is that since this format is acceptable as a URL address, you can make it into a bookmark like any other. Press Ctrl-B and bring up the full bookmark edit window. Create a new header called EMAIL and then add all your regular correspondents one by one, with their real names in the Name box and their mailto: addresses in the Location box. Now when you pull down your bookmark list, you'll be able to select "email" then "Julia" using just your keyboard arrow keys or your mouse. Perhaps one of these days you'll even be able to select your message to Julia from a pull-down menu!

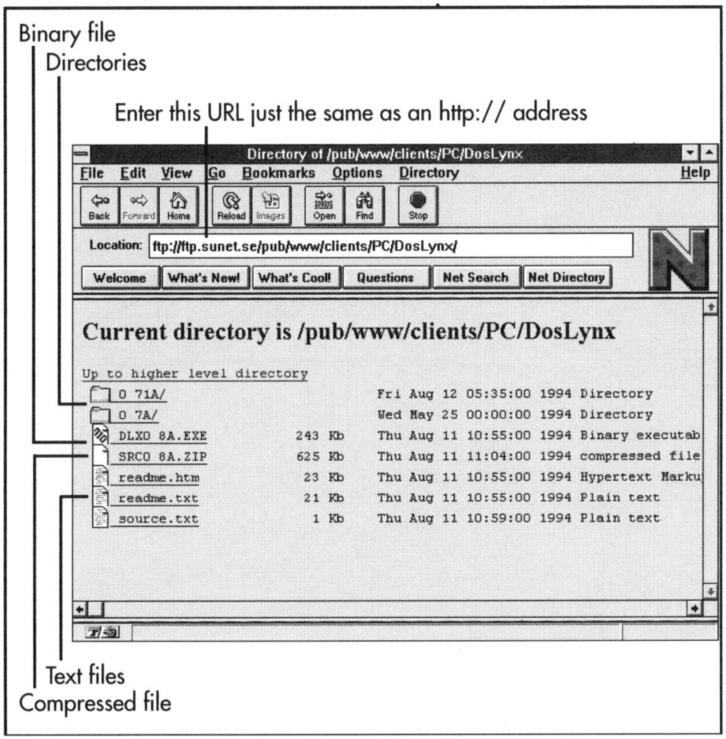
Binary file
Directories
Enter this URL just the same as an http:// address
Directory of /pub/www/clients/PC/DosLynx
File Edit View Go Bookmarks Options Directory Help
Back Forward Home Reload Images Open Find Stop
Location: ftp://ftp.sunet.se/pub/www/clients/PC/DosLynx/
Welcome What's New! What's Cool! Questions Net Search Net Directory
Current directory is /pub/www/clients/PC/DosLynx
Up to higher level directory
0 71A/ Fri Aug 12 05:35:00 1994 Directory
0 7A/ Wed May 25 00:00:00 1994 Directory
DLXO 8A.EXE 243 Kb Thu Aug 11 10:55:00 1994 Binary executab
SRCO 8A.ZIP 625 Kb Thu Aug 11 11:04:00 1994 compressed file
readme.htm 23 Kb Thu Aug 11 10:55:00 1994 Hypertext Marku
readme.txt 21 Kb Thu Aug 11 10:55:00 1994 Plain text
source.txt 1 Kb Thu Aug 11 10:59:00 1994 Plain text
Text files
Compressed file

Figure 4-13: *The file names in this FTP site directory act just like hypertext links—click 'em and grab 'em.*

FTP

Both of us are old enough net-jockeys to remember when anonymous FTP (File Transfer Protocol) was a real chore. There was a lot to type—with perfect accuracy—just to get connected. Directory listings would whiz by out of control; you'd have to remember to switch between ASCII and binary modes to get your downloads right; to inspect a README file, you'd have to pipe it through a separate UNIX pager; and in general the command set was about what you'd expect for one of the oldest forms of Internetting there is.

The first move in the direction of user-friendliness was the invention of the UNIX program ncftp, which at least logged on for you, remembered your favorite sites and directories, and provided a way of displaying all those README files. Today, Windows-based FTP applications easily handle automatic login, scrolling of directory listings, and README by mouse.

Netscape has one of the best FTP programs there is—it does all that, plus displaying directory listings with an icon accompanying each entry showing what type of file it is. When it comes to a download, you don't have to decide whether this is supposed to be binary or ASCII: Netscape knows already. When you click on a file icon, Netscape follows whatever instructions you have given it on how to handle file types (Preferences/Helper Applications). This will normally be "Display a text file—Save a binary to disk."

HOT TIP —·——·——·——·——·——·——·——·——·——·——·——·—

Keep a list of your often-visited FTP sites in a special bookmark subdirectory. Their URL addresses all begin "ftp://...." and often "ftp" appears twice in the complete address—for example **ftp://ftp.digital.com.**

—·——·——·——·——·——·——·——·——·——·——·——·—

Gopher

The Internet Gopher was always a much friendlier way of accessing what's out there: It actually reads many of the same data sources that FTP and TELNET and WAIS do, but it strips out the jargon and reduces everything to a menu choice. You can start anywhere and get anywhere from any starting point in the great labyrinth of Gopher-burrows. One good starting point is the "Gopher Jewels" menu maintained by the

University of Southern California. Its URL is

gopher://cwis.usc.edu:70/11 Other_Gophers_and_Information_ Resources/Gopher-Jewels

One difficulty we always had, when searching for something with the Gopher, was remembering which Gopher-burrows we had already explored: Netscape's color change for "followed links" applies as much to Gopher menu items as it does to Web pages, and it's a terrific help. So is the Back button.

In a sense, the philosophy of the Gopher, invented at the University of Minnesota, laid the groundwork for the World Wide Web by showing that Internet resources could be made accessible to the kind of people who did not care to learn FTP commands and never found out the difference between a binary and an ASCII file transfer. Now the Gopher may be a victim of the phenomenal success of the Web. One Gopher site we've used more times than we could count has just announced that it is going "out of business" in favor of a super-duper Web page.

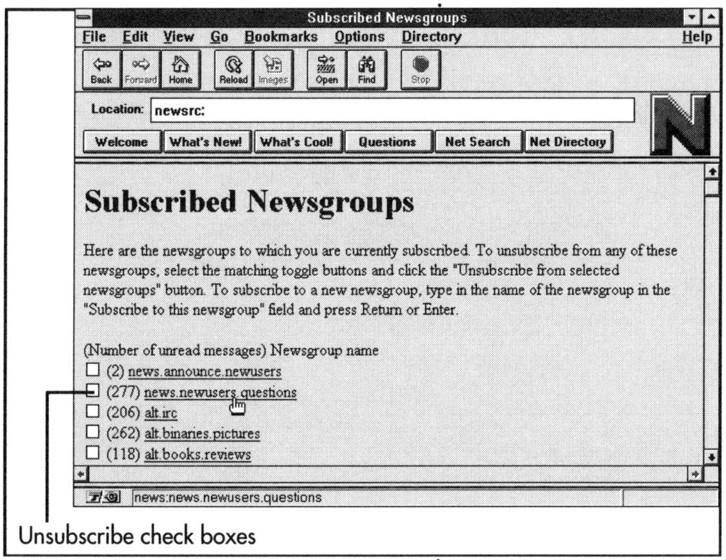

TELNET

Like Gopher, many of the services offered by TELNET are being revised these days into a more accessible Web format. The TELNET protocol is the one you use to connect your computer directly to another computer which may be in Australia as easily as in Washington DC.

We used to TELNET often to the library of Dartmouth College (**baker.dartmouth.edu**) to use their searchable Shakespeare to help with

Figure 4-14: *Netscape's main Newsgroup display.*

Unsubscribe check boxes

the cryptic crosswords we're addicted to. Now that we've discovered the hypertext Shakespeare (**http://the-tech.mit.edu/Shakespeare/works.html**), we won't be going to Dartmouth so often. However, TELNET is far from obsolete—if you ever need to do any serious database searching, you're going to get to know TELNET and the WAIS services TELNET can get you to.

Netscape needs helper software to complete a TELNET connection. One we use is QVTNET—a 32-bit Windows application obtainable from **ftp://ftp.iastate.edu/pub/pc/win3**. There are others. Whatever you choose, tell Netscape about it in the Preferences box and Directories, Applications and News.

USENET Newsgroups

You get to Netscape's newsreader from the Directory pull-down menu (or by keyboard Alt-D/G). However, before using this feature, refer to the note in Chapter 3 on Preferences/Directories, Applications and News. You'll need to tell Netscape the name of your NNTP server, and if you're already a case-hardened USENET freak, you may well be able to use your existing NEWSRC file (it's the file that keeps track of what newsgroups you like reading and what articles you've already read). If you don't give it a preexisting NEWSRC file to use, the first time you go to the Newsgroups, Netscape will kindly offer to create one for you. It will subscribe you to the three "newbie" newsgroups, **news.announce.newusers, news.newusers.questions**, and **news.answers**.

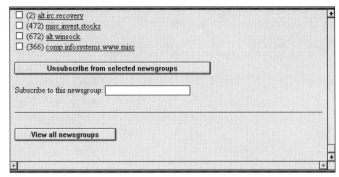

Figure 4-15: *Here's where you subscribe, unsubscribe or get the Big List.*

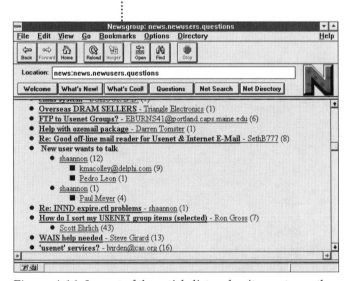

Figure 4-16: *Layout of the article list makes it easy to see the threads.*

Netscape's built-in newsreader is good. So good that we can't really do justice to all of its features in this book. Notice that number in parentheses between the "unsubscribe" check box and the newsgroup name? It's the number of unread articles in that group—you'd be amazed how very few newsreaders provide that information.

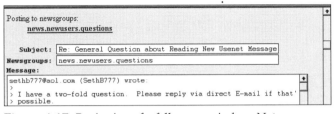

Figure 4-17: *Beginning of a follow-up window: Netscape practically writes it for you.*

Now click on one of the newsgroup names and see the layout of article titles. Once again, each article is accompanied by a count of the number of text lines in it. And all that indenting and subtitling is also a "deluxe" feature: This reader is what's known as "threaded," meaning that all articles on the same topic are grouped together.

Another fab feature that Netscape claims as unique (and we would not dispute the claim) is its ability to find and interpret hypertext links and HTML formatting in news articles. To see this, subscribe to one of the newsgroups that discusses the Web, like **comp.infosystems.www.misc** (you'll find Netscape announcements and bug discussions here). Many of the articles will be "signed" with a hypertext link to the author's home page, or contain links to images, other URLs, whatever HTML can provide. If you want to include HTML codes in a posting of your own, enclose a section of your article within the coding <HTML>.....</HTML>. But bear in mind that only Netscape users will see it as you intend.

Apart from those "hot" features of the newsreader, it also makes some routine newsreader functions like posting, following up and mailing to an article author very, very easy. Here's the screen you get for article follow-up, for instance:

To subscribe to a new newsgroup, it helps to know its full name so that you can simply write it in. To browse all newsgroups, you'll have to select the View All Newsgroups button in the main Newsgroup page, and downloading all those names takes a while. **Note:** If the View All Newsgroups button is absent in your version of Netscape, see Appendix A for an alternative. To unsubscribe to a group, you have two choices: (1) click on the check box beside that group in your main subscription list then select the Unsubscribe From Selected News-groups button, or (2) use the Unsub button at the top or the bottom of the list of articles in the group.

Archie

Archie is the Internet service that allows you to search every FTP site in the world for directory and file names containing a keyword that you're interested in—"beatle", let's say. Even though there's no such thing as a URL beginning "archie://...," this wonderful service is available on the Web thanks to a so-called hypertext "gateway" provided by NCSA.

Go to **http://hoohoo.ncsa.uiuc.edu/archie.html** and you'll find all the archie commands all wrapped up in one fill-out-and-submit Web page.

First is a box for you to enter your keyword or words. Then comes a pop-up menu of four different search types; the default is not case-sensitive and searches for the string, not the word (which means that *Beatles* would be found by searching for *beatle*). Radio buttons allow you to pick between a sort by Host computer or by Date. Another pop-up allows you to choose the "niceness" rating of your search— Not Nice at All/Nice/Nicer/Very Nice/Extremely Nice/Nicest. Archie servers are in demand, and

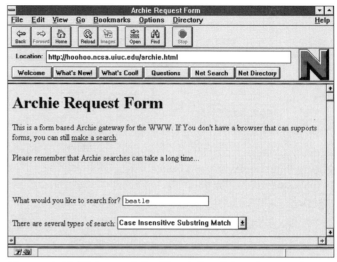

Figure 4-18: *This search for "beatle" took less than a minute and produced 33 files to choose from.*

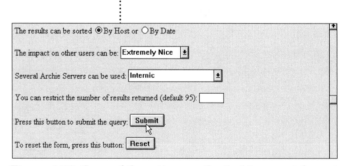

Figure 4-19: *Some of the options on the Archie request form at NCSA.*

there's always a queue of users waiting for search results. Niceness is basically a way of saying "After you—I insist" or "Do you mind?—I'm in a real hurry." If you accept the default "Very Nice," you will barge ahead of somebody who has rated her search "Nicest." (We're looking forward to the day when this menu comes up changed to Polite/Cool/Supercilious/Bloody Rude.) If you're not in a hurry and can do something else meanwhile, you might consider being Extremely Nice.

One more pop-up list is a selection of Archie servers. Pick one that's geographically close (Internic, a good one, is in California just a few miles from our office). Finally, you have options to restrict the search by domain and number of hits. All this to save you from having to compose a UNIX command like: **archie -s -m100 -N5000 beatle**

Searches can take a while—the nicer, the longer, obviously—but Netscape makes life very easy once the results are in. The hit list becomes a hypertext document which you can scroll, save or click on to go straight to the likeliest source of that Beatles lyric you were looking for. Truly luxurious search-and-grab.

Finger

The Department of Computer Science of the University of Indiana has kindly provided another hypertext "gateway"—this one to Finger services. Its address is **http://www.cs.indiana.edu/finger/**.

Finger was originally used in UNIX networks to find out who else is logged on, see when they last checked their e-mail , and consult project files created for that specific purpose. "Project files" has come to mean all sorts of weird things. Add **dmc.iris. washington.edu/spyder** onto Finger's address, and you'll get a readout of recent seismic events worldwide.

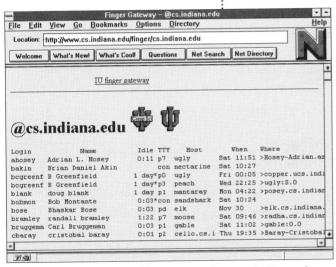

Figure 4-20: *Enter http://www.cs.indiana.edu/finger/ cs.indiana.edu to find out who's logged on at Indiana right now.*

California residents can get information about their Congressional representatives by fingering **sen.ca.gov/** followed by their ZIP Code. And then there's always the state of the Coca Cola machine at various US universities. Carnegie-Mellon (**coke.elab.cs.cmu.edu**) was the first to make their coke fingerable, and others have followed. Cyndi Williams provides weekly trivia by Finger at **magnus1.com/cyndiw**. There may also be baseball scores, weather forecasts, and Nielsen ratings out there in Finger-space—the sites change too frequently for a book to be a very reliable source of good Finger addresses.

In general, a user@host address needs to be formatted as host/user for the Indiana gateway. So to find out about someone whose e-mail address is **ualee@mcl.ucsb.edu**, you have to type:

http://www.cs.indiana.edu/finger/mcl.ucsb.edu/ualee

If you don't specify a user, you are likely to get a readout of everyone logged in to that host machine (see Figure 4-20).

The actual source of the information Finger conveys is the first line of a file called ".project," and the whole of a file called ".plan" (these conventions originated at UC Berkeley). One or both have to be present in the user's home directory. So if you want to provide some information of interest to somebody who Fingers you, you need to have a UNIX shell account and simply make up those files.

Staying Current

Just when you think you know everything and are all up to speed, it's bound to happen. New connection services, software updates, new protocols and standards—they'll all come pouring at you, and before you know it you're behind the times again.

Just by checking in to the Web and using its resources regularly you'll undoubtedly stay apprised of the most significant developments.

But here are some places where you can check to find out what's new on the Web and what new geewhizzery is just around the corner.

Getting Updates

Announcements about new updates to Netscape are posted on the Netscape Communications Corporation's home page (access via the Directory menu—Netscape Communications Corporation). You can also find out about updates to Netscape, as well as to your TCP/IP stack and helper applications, by staying abreast of the newsgroups on Web browsers and reading the recent FAQs.

FAQs & Other Reading Material

Besides Netscape's own online FAQ (accessed via the directory button Questions or Menu bar-Help-Frequently Asked Questions), there are several good FAQs for newsgroups concerned with the Web and Web browsers. They can all be found in Web-browser format in the USENET FAQ archive at Ohio State:

http://www.cis.ohio-state.edu/hypertext/faq/usenet/FAQ-List.html

A particularly useful FAQ is the comp.infosystems.www FAQ, which you can also find at **http://sunsite.unc.edu/boutell/faq/www_faq.html**

Another good introductory guide to the Web is the WWW Primer, found at **http://www.vuw.ac.nz/who/Nathan.Torkington/ideas/www-primer.html**

Information Sites

The WWW Information Site is a good place to start for Web-related information. It has links to several different topics for users, service providers and Web authors. You can find it at:

http://www.bsdi.com/server/doc/web-info.html

Scott Yanoff's famous "Special Internet Connections," always a reliable and up-to-date guide to what's good, is now available as a hypertext document at

http://www.uwm.edu/Mirror/inet.services.html

Newsgroups

Several newsgroups are dedicated to exchanging information about Web browsers. They're a good place to ask questions or look for solutions to problems you may have, and also to stay abreast of the latest updates. Some that we've found particularly useful are

comp.infosystems.www.misc

comp.infosystems.www.providers

comp.infosystems.www.users

comp.infosystems.announce

alt.winsock

alt.internet.services

Netscape Corporation designers often check into these newsgroups to monitor and volunteer information.

Moving On

By now you should be aware that the Web is all things to all people. Perhaps you're still just enjoying exploring, or maybe you've found your own little niche of favorite sites run by like-minded Web users. Maybe you're feeling like you'd like to stake your claim on a little patch in this frontier.

In the next chapter we'll tell you how to do that. We'll tell you a bit about Web page design and start you off on designing a simple page in HTML. Your imagination and ambition can take off from there.

MAKING YOUR OWN WEB DOCUMENTS

In Chapter 3 you saw how Netscape actually creates a personal Web page for you with the Bookmark menu. It only takes a little imagination to wonder whether you couldn't personalize it a little—say, insert your own picture and some info you'd like to include about yourself—and save it as a home page file.

We'll show you how. So that you understand all the basics of HTML composition, we'll start fresh and design a complete Web page with in-line images and hypertext links. You'll be able to copy any of our techniques for yourself—and we'll give you detailed instructions on how to exploit the New Age of Plagiarism.

HTML: The Language of the Web

Go to a Web page—any old page will do—and pick the menu choice View/Source. What you see is HTML. Look scary? Awww, c'mon—it's not like a real computer language. At least you can see some ordinary

English text in there (okay, if you picked a Spanish site you can see Spanish).

Mixed in with the text, sometimes quite densely, are a lot of things like <H1>, </H1>, <P>, </P>, <A HREF="file">, and so on. Those are just the tags that the Web browser needs to interpret the author's page. In general, they come in pairs such as <H1> for a start tag, </H1> for an end tag. Some HTML authors use lowercase letters—some use a mixture of uppercase and lowercase. Frankly, my dear, the Web doesn't give a damn.

An entire HTML document is (usually) enclosed within a tag pair, like this:

<HTML> ....everything in the document
</HTML>

It needs to be subdivided once only, like this:

<HTML>
<HEAD>
....everything in the header: Title, document type, etc.
</HEAD>
<BODY>
....everything in the body (in other words, everything that's actually going to appear on the page).
</BODY>
</HTML>

Starting with that simple framework, which you can see in Figure 5-1, we're going to build a home page for you visually, explaining each new element as we add it.

Building a Home Page

The way we normally work is to have our HTML text file in Notepad (or any text editor) in the left two-thirds of the screen, and Netscape up (but not connected to the Net) in the right two-thirds of the screen. They overlap but can be brought into the foreground just by clicking. The local file is loaded into Netscape initially by the menu choice File/ Open File, or Ctrl-O. We use the Reload toolbar button or Ctrl-R thereafter. After each change we make to the HTML file, we Save the file and Reload the page into Netscape to see what effect our change has had. We always use the file extension .htm, although Netscape does not check files at the door and turn away any that aren't named correctly.

All of the text we want to put in our Web page is defined first as paragraphs. Every paragraph begins with <P> and ends with </P>. HTML ignores all line breaks and carriage returns in a source file, and only creates a line break when it sees </P>. In Figure 5-2, you can see how all of the basic text in our page is set up in eight paragraphs.

Next we'd like to make a proper list out of our travel diary entries. We'll choose the <OL> tag, for an Ordered List. We could have picked <DL>Definition List, <UL>Unordered list, <MENU> or others. We replace the <P> at the beginning of our list text with <OL> and the </P> at the end with </OL>. Then we encase each element in the list within the <LI>...</LI> codes (for List Item). We don't need to add the numbers—Netscape will do that. The results are shown in Figure 5-3.

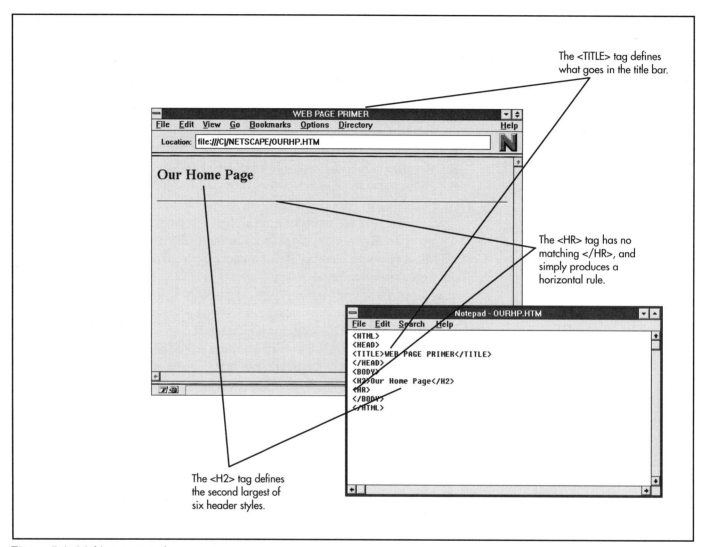

The <TITLE> tag defines what goes in the title bar.

The <HR> tag has no matching </HR>, and simply produces a horizontal rule.

The <H2> tag defines the second largest of six header styles.

Figure 5-1: *Making a start: three new tags.*

This word will be
replaced with a picture.

The <EM> </EM> tags
add emphasis to the
word "really."

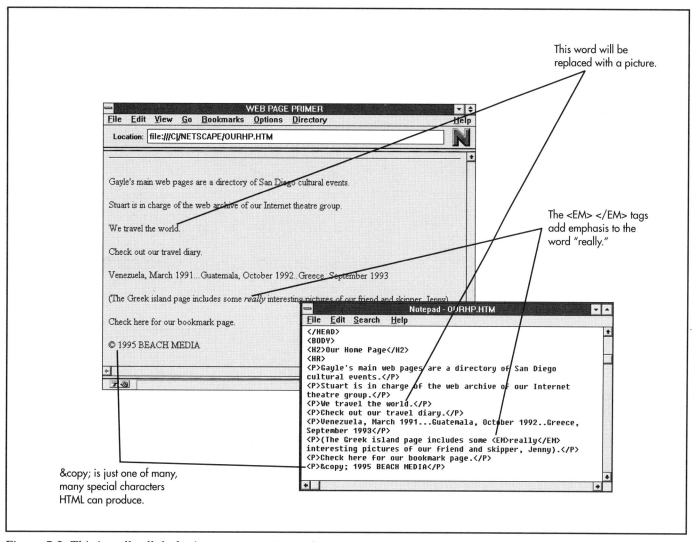

© is just one of many,
many special characters
HTML can produce.

Figure 5-2: *This is really all the basic text we want to put in.*

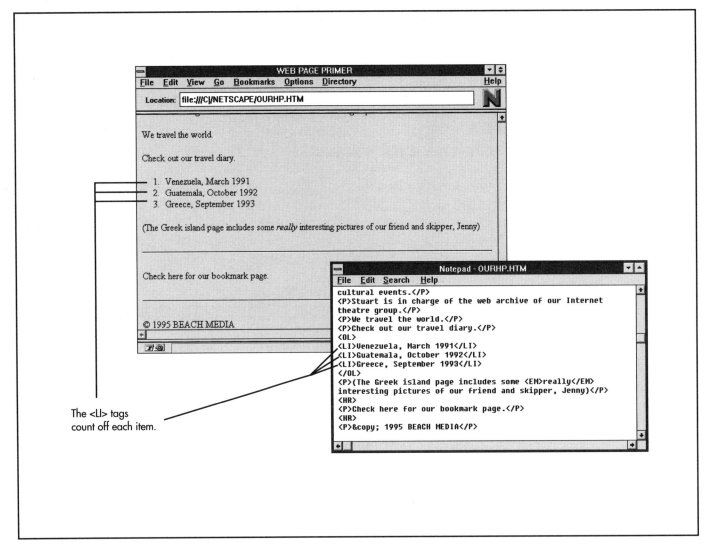

The <LI> tags
count off each item.

Figure 5-3: *Making a proper list.*

Adding Images & Links

As we mentioned before (Chapter 4), in-line "thumbnail" images must be in the .GIF format (actually .XBM and .XPM are allowed, but everybody uses .GIF). If you don't have your own scanner to scan in your favorite holiday snapshots, you'll need to find either a friend with a scanner (such people are getting more and more popular) or a lab that can do it. The lab people will try and blind you with science, but your requirement is simple and straightforward: you need a full-screen color .GIF with the best resolution possible given that you do not want to end up with a data file bigger than, say, 75k. (The size of the file will be much reduced after you crop it and size it for an in-line .GIF.) Anything bigger has more definition than anybody will ever see and will simply make the page slow to load. One service we've used charges $9.95 and they shoot in 24 hours—or faster for more money.

You're going to need some image management software (LVIEW works fine for this) to allow you to do your own cropping and sizing. You can play all kinds of fancy games keeping icon libraries and in-line directories, but for the sake of simplicity let's assume the complete kit—the HTML file plus all hypermedia files—is in the Netscape directory.

So, once you've got the .GIFs all cropped, sized and assembled, you call each of them into your page with the tag
<IMG SRC = "filename.GIF">. You can see the results in Figure 5-4.

That's already nice, but a couple of adjustments to the "World" in-line are in order. First, it would be nice if the middle of the image lines up with the text rather than the bottom. Second, if we intend to post our page on the Web, we have to bear in mind that not everyone is seeing this page in a graphical Web browser. There are perfectly good—and very fast—text browsers. Lynx is the most popular.

Lynx users, if we don't help them out, will see that line as

We travel the [IMAGE]

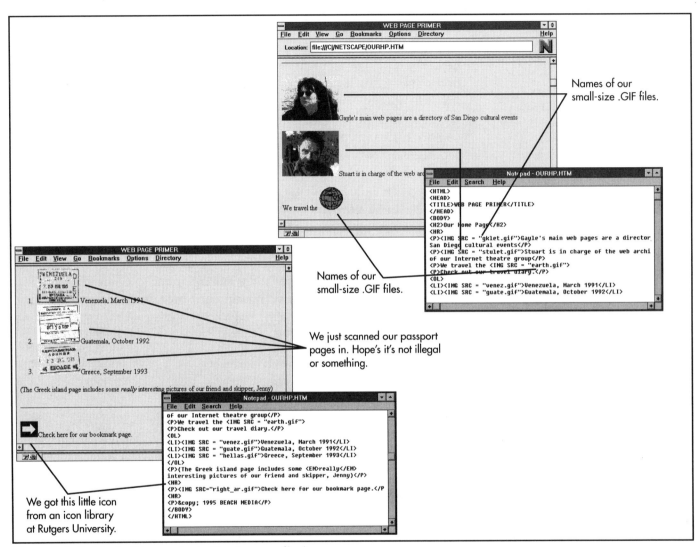

Figure 5-4: *Suddenly this page is starting to come alive!*

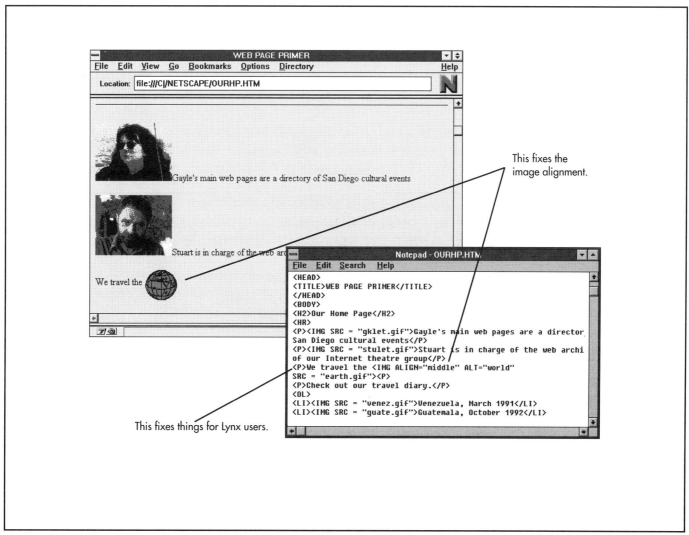

Figure 5-5: *Fixing a couple of little problems*

The way to help them out is to make use of the tag ALT, meaning "If you can't show an image, here's what to replace it with." If you're making your page just for your own use, of course, you needn't bother.

Links

Well, this is supposed to be hypertext, right? It's time we hypered off to some other destinations.

A hypertext link (we'll just call it a link from now on) is signaled by two elements combined. The first is an anchor in the form <A> ...something... </A>, where the something is the word or picture that the user will click on to activate the link. The second is a reference in the form HREF="...something...", and in this case the something is where the link leads to: a different part of this document, another document, an external image or other hypermedia event, or a URL address on a completely different computer possibly in a different country.

One document we're definitely going to need to link to is our travel diary, which is a separate document in our own computer called "trdiary.htm." To turn the word "Venezuela" into a link to its part of "trdiary.htm" we write the combined tags like this:

<A HREF="trdiary.htm#Lagunetas">Venezuela</A>

That "#Lagunetas" tagged on to the file name tells Netscape to go to the internal label "Lagunetas" which is buried somewhere in "trdiary.htm."

Now, if we take a look at the top half of the page, we'll see that the in-line .GIFs themselves can be made into links. It's just a matter of wrapping the <A HREF="filename">Hyperlink Text</A> around everything correctly.

Note that the full-size "external" pictures can be any format, and many are in regular use on the Web. It explains why Netscape's Preferences-Helper Applications dialog box is so complicated.

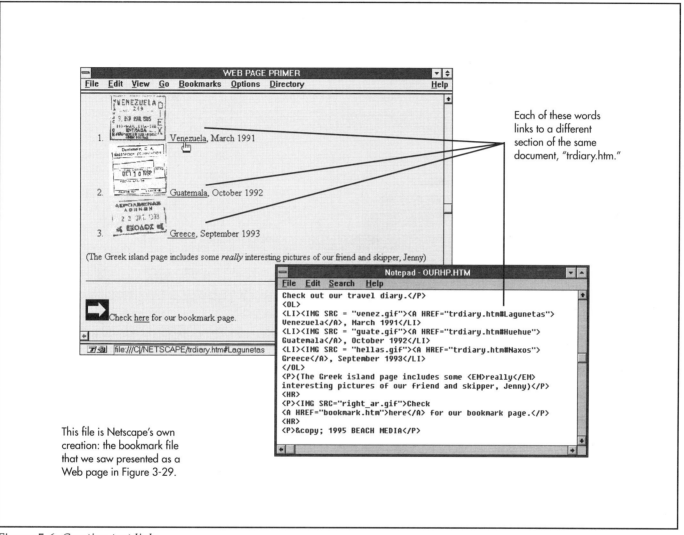

Each of these words links to a different section of the same document, "trdiary.htm."

This file is Netscape's own creation: the bookmark file that we saw presented as a Web page in Figure 3-29.

Figure 5-6: *Creating text links.*

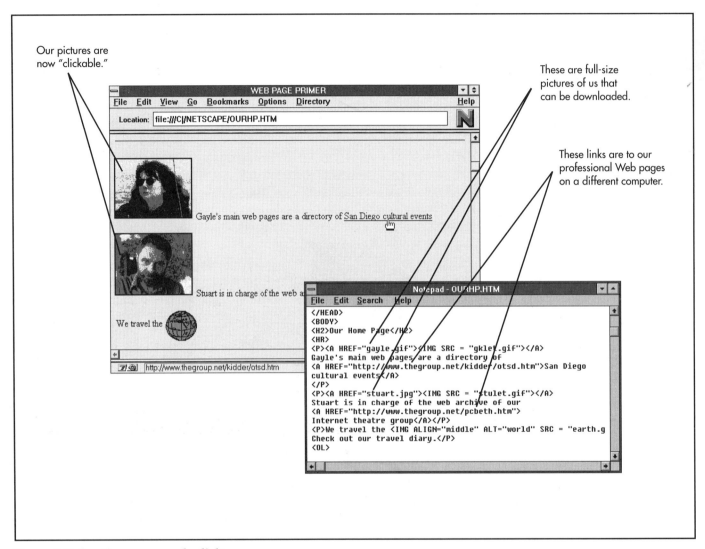

Figure 5-7: *Creating more complex links.*

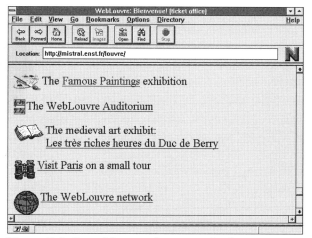

Figure 5-8: *Something caught our eye in the WebLouvre....*

Figure 5-9: *The little icon we decided to steal.*

How We Raided the Louvre— And They'll Never Catch Us!

Remember how we mentioned, back in Chapter 3, that the Web is a free-for-all that makes copyright attorneys wake up screaming in the night? And back in Chapter 4, the fact that the Louvre museum pages are renowned for good design? Put those two facts together and you have the background to a daringly successful raid we carried out on the Louvre one day.

We were wondering how to draw an icon to use as a link to our travel diary when we saw the Louvre page depicted in Figure 5-8. "What nice in-line .GIFs," we thought. And then we thought, just like many art thieves must have thought, "Hmmm... would look swell in our collection." Figure 5-9 shows what we were after.

So we waited until the dead of night, Paris time (it helped that they were eight hours ahead), and then returned to that Web page. Moving silently but efficiently, we stroked our mouse pointer oh-so-gently against the Menu item View/Source. It took but a second's scrolling time to find the key we were looking for, all unguarded in the plain light of the View Source window. Figure 5-10 shows what a simple matter it is to locate that line in the HTML source document that gives the game away: **img src="/louvre/gif/earth.gif."** Aha! So, the cunning devils have concealed their collection of .GIF files in a subdirectory called **louvre/gif**, have they? Clever... but not clever enough to throw us off.

Working quickly now, afraid to hear the words *"mais, Monsieur et Madame... ooh la-la! Qu'est-ce que vous faites?"* we pulled up our Preferences-Helper Applications dialog box. Normally "image-gif" has "Netscape" in its Action column, because we want Netscape to show us .GIF images. But it took a second to change that to "Save," to set the stage for the final act of larceny.

Back in the main window, we put a cursor at the right-hand end of the URL window and added "**/gif/ earth.gif**" onto the WebLouvre's URL. A touch to the Enter key, and the prize was ours. All that remained was to decide, as Figure 5-11 shows, what to call our booty. We settled on the default "earth.gif," and the rest you know.

Testing Your Page

As you can see, we've composed our page using nothing but a simple text editor (Windows Notepad), and for simple Web page design you need nothing more. However, fancier Web page design can get much more complicated, and it's often hard to remember to put all the right code in the right places. Those who get serious about Web page design generally find that HTML editors are worthwhile to simplify the job and reduce frustration.

One we've used frequently is HoTMetaL. As you're composing, HoTMetaL will prompt you for the appropriate codes and let you know if you're violating rules of HTML composition. Even when we've composed our page with a text editor and it looks good on Netscape, we find it good practice to test the page by loading it into HoTMetaL. (See Figure 5-12.) If HoTMetaL finds something wrong, it won't load it and will tell you what it thinks the problem is. There's a good chance that if HoTMetaL has problems, another Web browser will have problems too.

If you intend to post your page for public access on the Web, it's important to remember that not everyone on the Web has Netscape.

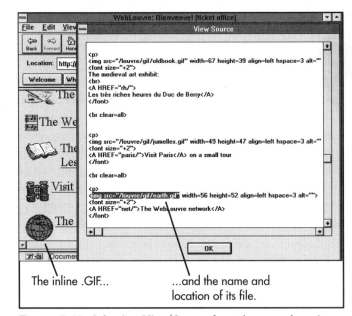

The inline .GIF...   ...and the name and location of its file.

Figure 5-10: *Selecting View/Source from the menu bar gives away the inside dope.*

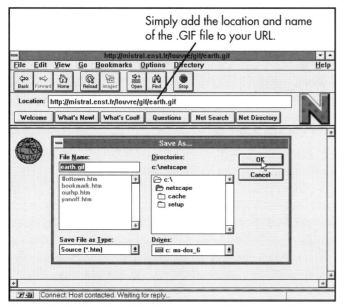

Figure 5-11: *"earth.gif" is about to be added to our private collection...*

Netscape is very forgiving, but some other Web browsers can be very particular. If at all possible, you should try viewing your page with other browsers (such as Mosaic and Cello). You should also consider the users without graphical interfaces who will see your page as pure text. You can test-view your page with the textual browser, Lynx, which you can access online. It's also a good idea to see what it looks like on different machines.

Of course, all of this is irrelevant if you've just designed your page for your own amusement and private use (and you can always send it to friends). For truly professional Web page design, you should engage a professional. Accessing databases, devising proper forms for two-way information, and ensuring security is a whole 'nother kettle of fish.

Posting Your Page

So you think the whole world should know about the wonderful page you've just designed, huh? The spirit of the Internet, after all, is that anyone can participate and there are no taste arbiters deciding who can and can't be part of it. Practically speaking, though, posting your page for public access is a lot more complicated on the World Wide Web, unless you're hooked up to a major academic or big business server—in which case all anyone needs is your URL address to get to your page.

If your page falls in the nature of public service—information that other people might conceivably like to use—you may find a community bulletin board that would like to include it in their postings or an access provider who is willing to post it free to enhance his or her own service.

If your page has a business or commercial aspect, there are plenty of access providers who would be happy to post it for you for a fee, and given the competitive nature of the business right now, the fees can be quite reasonable. Web business is a lively, developing field—check around and see what you can turn up.

Web Page Design Tips

Good Web page design is largely a matter of common sense. Nothing is more irritating to Web browsers than coming across a huge document with multiple links and numerous in-line images that takes several minutes to download onto your system before you discover that it's not what you want at all.

Some useful things to remember:

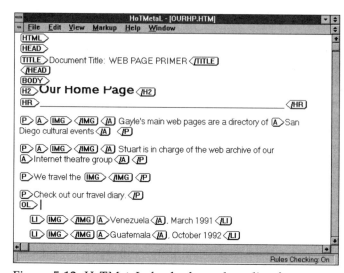

Figure 5-12: *HoTMetaL clearly shows the coding for our page.*

- Close all your statements—every <X> needs a </X> with a few exceptions (such as <HR> and <IMG>).

- Keep your in-line images small—under 25k is a good guide. All six of the little in-line images we used in our demonstration page totalled less than 50k, and the page loads in a few seconds.

- Offer a link to larger images and if they're very large files (over 75k), tell readers how large they are.

- Break large documents into smaller files logically. They'll load faster and be easier to use.

- Make sure your hyperlinks have full addresses.

- Test your page and all its links. If possible, test it with different browsers and on different kinds of machines.

- Describe your document accurately in the Title, and resist the

Online HTML Editing Guides Anyone interested in delving further into HTML composition can find lots of HTML guides and reference material on the Web. For the authoritative information, go straight to HTML's birthplace at the European Laboratory for Particle Physics (CERN), where the father of HTML himself, Tim Berners-Lee, has posted the HTML Style Guides, as well as a number of other HTML reference documents.

http://info.cern.ch/hypertext/WWW/ Provider/Style/Overview.html

A good HTML FAQ can be found at

http://sunsite.unc.edu/boutell/faq www_faq.html

You can create simple HTML documents online and save them to your own computer with the EasyHTML editor at:

http://peachpit.ncsa.uiuc.edu:80/easyhtml/

WebLint, another online HTML editing aid, will check any HTML document you've created for coding problems and let you know what you should do to fix it. Its address is:

http://www.unipress.com/web lint

temptation to be too cute. The title is frequently used by Web searchers to find topics on the Web.

- Keep it simple. As in all good design, less is more.

Moving On

You may not realize it, but what you've actually learned in this chapter is HTML Plus, the newest version of the language of the Web. With the simple basics we've given you we hope you'll have fun creating your own documents. If nothing else, it could be a great party showoff—and perhaps slightly more entertaining than home videos of your latest trip (depending on your taste).

In the next chapter we'll talk about some specialized Web applications. We'll dig into the wealth of reference materials available on the Web and toss up some of the more useful gems. We'll look at the various search engines and how you can find out what's available on the Web on any topic you're interested in. And finally, we'll give you some more neat pages you can visit as you continue your journeys on the Web with Netscape Navigator.

SPECIAL APPLICATIONS & SITES

Now that you've had a chance to see what the Web has to offer, it's highly likely you're eager to find your own particular interests—be they recreational, business or research oriented. Finding that special something is not always an easy job, particularly because the Web changes every day.

Much of this chapter we'll devote to the task of searching the Web. We'll explain what kind of searches you can do and how to construct a search. Then we'll look at what some of our favorite search engines do and compare their results.

Then it's time for some more Web-sailing. We'll leave you with a list of our favorite Web sites—prize-winning pages, repositories of great information, or just-plain-fun stuff.

Web Searching Tips

The first thing to realize about search engines on the Web is that not all searchers are created equal. The types of data they look for and the kinds of searches they do can be very different. One searcher may look for keywords in the titles of documents only, another will search all hypertext citation links in documents for the keyword. Still a third will search the entire text of the documents in its base.

In the latter case, you can see how a lot of irrelevant information can be thrown up. This is especially so if it is searching for a string instead of a word. Say you typed in "bee" for a keyword. If it's searching for the string it will find "beer" and "has-been" and "beetroot" and who-knows-what-all.

Another difference in search engines is the extent to which they allow you to qualify your search, since obviously the more you can qualify it, the better your chances of getting exactly what you want. Most searchers encourage you to put as many keywords as you think relevant in your search, but this is not always helpful—it may simply turn up more irrelevant documents rather than relevant ones.

Here are the basic types of searches possible. Bear in mind that not all searchers are capable of all of them.

- Simple keyword search

  killer bee

  This will return all documents containing either the word "killer" or "bee."

- Boolean query

  bee AND killer

  This looks for occurrences of both words in a document, in any order.

- Phrase query

  "killer bee"

This will return all documents that contain "killer bee" as a phrase.

You can devise even more complex searches, such as:

- Boolean queries with phrases

  "killer bee" AND California

- Simple structured query

  Title: "killer bee"

This will only return documents that have "killer bee" in the Title.

- Complex query

  California AND (Title: "killer bee")

No matter what you do, expect a few surprises. When we tried this out, our search for "killer bee" threw up, unexpectedly, a rock band called The Killer Bees and a NASA computer dubbed the killerbee.

The basic things to keep in mind when searching are

- Know what kind of citations the searcher is looking for. Read the Help screens and FAQs before you start.

- Be as specific as you can.

- Use OR to widen your search. Use AND to narrow it.

- Don't use words that are too general or too common. The documentation for one Web searcher points out that "to be or not to be" is reduced to nothing by its initial keyword processing.

- Don't use plural forms or weird declensions.

- Realize that sometimes all it takes is a few good hits, as similar documents on a subject may well link to each other.

- Remember where you've been. Take notes if necessary.

Our Favorite Web Searchers

One of the most-thumbed sections of our bookmark list, in Mosaic and Lynx as well as Netscape, is the "Web Searchers" list. Like everyone else, we have research needs both formal (providing biology abstracts for non-net-savvy clients) and informal (what was that address for the Paris Metro route planner?).

There are dozens of Web searchers available for your use, several of which you can find referenced on your Net Search directory button. To review our favorite searchers in some coherent way for this book, we gave them the task of searching for a commodity we love—French wine.

The WebCrawler

Possibly our favorite searcher because it's so easy and quick, the Crawler's at the University of Washington:

**http://webcrawler.cs.washington.edu/
WebCrawler/WebQuery.html**

(and you'd better get all those capital letters correct).

Figure 6-1 shows the Crawler's inquiry screen with that check box we love, to switch between an AND search and an OR search, plus the pull-down that limits the search if we just want a start point rather than the full reference desk treatment.

The Crawler does not search the Web itself when you ask it about French wine (or anything else). Instead it searches its own *index* of the

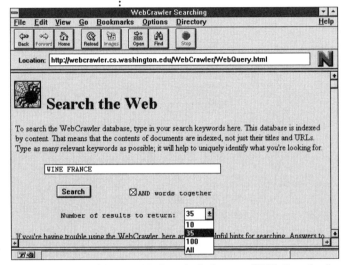

Figure 6-1: *Washington University's famous "WebCrawler."*

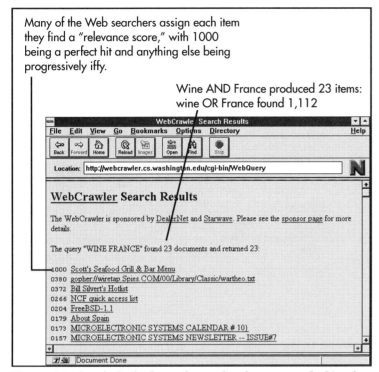

Many of the Web searchers assign each item they find a "relevance score," with 1000 being a perfect hit and anything else being progressively iffy.

Wine AND France produced 23 items: wine OR France found 1,112

Figure 6-2: *Scott's Seafood wasn't exactly what we were looking for, but item 3 eventually led to gold.*

Web—a database of about 100mb that indexes nearly 400,000 documents. Our one beef about the Crawler is that this index is not updated as often as we (and other Web citizens) would like. The massive update may happen only every three months, and a lot can happen in three months on the Web.

Harvest

There are two main URL addresses for the Harvest system: The first is more available and the second is more thorough.

http://www.town.hall.org/brokers/www-home-pages/query.html

http://harvest.cs.colorado.edu/brokers/www-home-pages/query.html

Why, you may ask, do they call themselves "brokers"? The answer is that these sites call in other searchers to aid them. The **town.hall** site uses a WAIS (Wide Area Information Service) indexer, which is efficient but weak when it comes to complex structured queries. The most powerful engine used is the Glimpse indexer at Arizona, which can even (sometimes) do a successful search on a misspelled keyword. Harvest's user-amicable features are its huge entry window and, especially, the format of its results lists. Our wine query produced 49 hits, of which this was the first:

1. filename: http://www.ifi.uio.no/~dash/wine/
   host: www.ifi.uio.no
   path: /~dash/wine/
   Description: The Wine project
   Content Summary

Everything underlined is a hypertext link, including that wonderful "Content Summary" that told us immediately that the "Wine project" was not the unfrozen concoction that helps us hang on, but a software interface between Windows and UNIX X-11 systems. A typical Web-searching debacle , actually.

Lycos

http://lycos.cs.cmu.edu

The Washington WebCrawler was not only our favorite in terms of convenience, but also the best—until Lycos came along. Lycos—a whole array of hardware and software at Carnegie-Mellon University, Pittsburgh, is super-duper. Like the Crawler, it keeps its own local index for search speed, but it also fetches new documents "on the fly" and adds them into its ever-burgeoning indexes. The larger of the two principal catalogs indexed its millionth URL in November 1994.

Okay, Lycos is a little bit slower than the Crawler—but it is much more thorough. It found so many citations for French wine that we dared to test it on the focus of our personal wine interest: the Burgundy region of France. In less than a minute Lycos gave us 36 citations for "burgundy" (see Figure 6-3) and in less than another minute twelve more for "bourgogne." Neither Harvest nor the Worm had found anything on those keywords. Probably it helps that one of Carnegie-Mellon's computers is actually called burgundy.

Lycos has the interesting philosophy of scoring a citation higher if it comes up in the first paragraph of a document. It is also superior when it comes to Boolean and limited search strings. If you enter "bee." it will understand that you want only honey producers, not beetles,

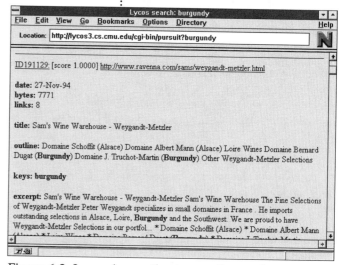

Figure 6-3: *Lycos gives us the story on Burgundy.*

beetroots or frisbees. It even allows "negative keyword" searching—so that, for instance, "ball -ball." would find "ballistic" but not "ball" itself.

World Wide Web Worm (WWWW)

http://www.cs.colorado.edu/home/mcbryan/WWWW.html

The Worm's big feature is its click-box that you can use to make a choice between searching hypertext, document titles, document names or substrings of URL addresses. It's one of the speediest searchers there is. And although it struck out on "burgundy," it was informative on wine more generally, even providing us with a wine map of Slovenia (some Slovenian has obviously invested hours in using the Web to promote the wines of the region, since it has popped up frequently).

The Worm claims technical superiority in its acceptance of so-called "regular expressions." These are not "regular" as opposed to "with all the trimmings, heavy on the mayo," but formatted strings containing things like wildcards. DOS users know these because they use them for copying families of similarly named files, like *.TXT. In keyword searching, a wildcard can be as simple as an asterisk standing in for any string, such as 9*, meaning all ZIP Codes beginning with 9. However, the Worm's capabilities go way beyond that, and beyond the reach of most casual users of the Web.

The CUI W3 Catalog

http://cui_www.unige.ch/w3catalog

CUI is very different from the other searchers we've chosen to feature in this chapter. It's almost like an index of abstracts—well, actually, that's *exactly* what it's like. Strange that it should have been the Centre Universitaire Informatique in Geneva that provided this, since it's virtually all in the English language. Its proximity to the region of

Burgundy helps it not at all when it comes to searching that keyword. But exhaustive Web searches are not CUI's game at all. Instead of searching the Web, it searches *indexes* of the Web, plagiarizing shamelessly the work of such toilers as Scott Yanoff and John December. The end result is a series of chatty little notations, each one providing a hypertext link to its source, which can be very useful indeed for certain levels of research.

The Great Burgundy Quest

This quick review was *not* a proper benchmark test, giving a hard-and-fast comparison of performance. We've tried, rather, to indicate what horses suit what courses and set up your expectations as well as possible.

You might wonder, though, what we finally came up with on burgundy wine. On wine, the Lycos hitlist, though accurate, actually did not lead to anything too interesting. Our best stuff came from picking the third item from the Crawler, Bill Silvert's Hotlist, and following that to the "Wine Home Page." That was nice but all-American, so we followed the link to "other wine pages" and ended up on the doorstep of our net-buddy Gary "Gazza" Hunt, whose funky home page is shown in Figure 4-12 of this book. We already knew Gazza to be a wine buff and secretary of the wine society of the University of Bath, England. However, there was nothing immediately Burgundian at Bath, so we followed Gazza's link back to the USA, to a wine newsletter called *GrapeVine*, which in turn offered a link to the USENET

Example of a CUI Web Catalog Entry   October 14, 1994: Forest Hill Vineyard is now on the WWW. Forest Hill Vineyard is one of the most distinguished California vineyards, producing their award-winning chardonnay. Perfect for dinners, gifts, and to say 'congratulations' or 'I love you'. **(nwn)**
Note: The link "nwn" takes you to "NCSA What's New"—the same place you'll get to using Netscape's What's New directory button.

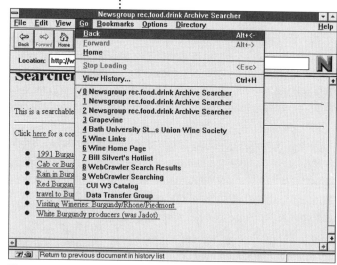

Figure 6-4: *Following the trail to Burgundy.*

newsgroup archives "rec.food.drink," yet another keyword search window, and finally seven good articles. Figure 6-4 shows the history list.

Prizewinning Web Pages

Web page design is fast becoming an art these days. How to balance visual presentation with good information and what kinds of information to include all need careful weighing. No doubt in your cruises so far you've found some good and bad examples and are beginning to form your own opinions on the subject.

Here, in no particular order, are some of the design contest winners, along with our own favorites. You'll find links to all of them in our *Netscape Quick Tour Online Companion* at **http://www.vmedia.com/nqt.html**.

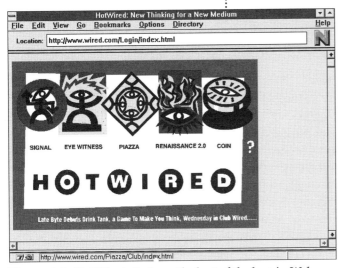

Figure 6-5: *HotWired: Perhaps the best of the best in Web graphics—and they take advertising, too.*

The Best of the Web

This is the home of the annual Best of the Web Contest which awards Web page designers for outstanding presentations in more than a dozen categories. You'll find links to all the winners as well as runners-up here. It's a great place to see what the state of the art in Web design is these days.
http://wings.buffalo.edu/contest/awards/index.html

Global Network Navigator

O'Reilly & Associates, pioneers in the Web, present a wealth of resources on the net on their extensive home pages, which include links to business pages, net news, travel, personal finance—and their own picks of the best of the Web.

http://gnn.com/gnn/gnn.html
Or got to **http://gnn.com** to become a registered subscriber.

ArtServe

Australian National University offers a comprehensive overview of their collections focusing on Art History. Access to some 2,800 images of prints, from the 15th century to the 19th century, including some 2,500 images of classical architecture and sculpture from around the Mediterranean.

http://rubens.anu.edu.au/

London's Natural History Museum

A heavy-duty site but why not? It's one of the major museums in the world, the home of Charles Darwin and friends. Extensive information on the museum's science programs and collections on earth and life sciences and the flora and fauna of MesoAmerica, among other things.

http://www.nhm.ac.uk/

The Virtual Hospital

The University of Iowa hospital has put a considerable amount of patient information online here for public access. Get information about heart disease, poison control, obstetrics and gynecology, sexually transmitted diseases and the warning signs of heart attack and stroke.

http://vh.radiology.uiowa.edu/Pt.Instr.Materials/PtInstruct.html

Travels With Samantha

MIT programmer Phil Greenspun's travelogue of his trip around North America with his PowerBook, Samantha, won a Best of the Web '94 award, as much for his beautiful pictures as his personal-style narrative. Be forewarned that you'll need considerable memory to view his high-quality images.

http://www.swiss.ai.mit.edu/samantha/travels-with-samantha.html

The Constitution of the United States of America

Want to check on your Constitutional rights? The entire Constitution is easily accessible online, thanks to Cornell University Law School.
http://www.law.cornell.edu/constitution/constitution.overview.html

Expo

Tour six expositions organized by the Library of Congress, with links to other major museum sites via the virtual shuttle bus. See the Soviet Archive Exhibit, the 1492 Exhibit, the Paleontology Exhibit, the Vatican Exhibit, the Dead Sea Scrolls Exhibit or the Spalato Exhibit exploring the palace of Diocletian at Split.
http://sunsite.unc.edu/expo/expo/busstation.html

Restaurant Le Cordon Bleu

The Restaurant Le Cordon Bleu is a sidestop on the virtual tour of museums above. A pictorial gourmet menu for each day of the week, with accompanying recipes from the cookbook "Le Cordon Bleu at Home."
http://sunsite.unc.edu/expo/restaurant/restaurant.html

The Virtual Tourist

Here you can find virtual tourist guides for countries around the world, as well as a link to a U.S. city guide index called City Net. Just click on the world map to see what's available.
http://wings.buffalo.edu/world/

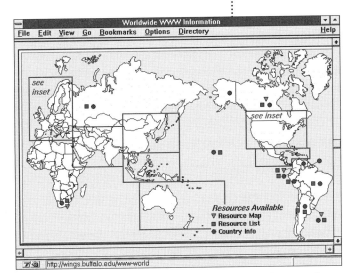

Figure 6-6: *If only travel were this easy.... nah, the agony's half the fun.*

Welcome to the Globewide Network Academy

Eventually you may be able to earn a degree online. Why not, if you can do it by mail? This unique site is the first cyberuniversity, a project by a consortium of educational and research organizations dedicated to devising a complete online university.

http://uu-gna.mit.edu:8001/uu-gna/

Arctic Adventours, Inc.

This Norwegian tour company advertizes their expeditions to the Arctic area aboard the yacht Arctic Explorer at this site. Lots of stunning pictures of Northern Norway, Siberia, and nameless icebergs.

http://www.oslonett.no/data/adv/AA/AA.html

The Branch Mall

The Branch Mall is one of the largest and longest established Internet Malls, with wares ranging from flowers and tee shirts to computer parts. Branch's success has been featured in the *New York Times, Inc Magazine, Money* and PBS Television.

http://www.branch.com:1080/index.html

The Hypertext Webster

An online searchable index of the Webster's dictionary. Look up any word and get the definition. If you spell it wrong, it will guess at what you mean and prompt you. Definitions are themselves hypertext-linked.

http://c.gp.cs.cmu.edu:5103/prog/webster?/

Current Weather Maps/Movies

The definitive site for weather maps and information. Find out the weather anywhere in the world and view the latest satellite pictures.

http://clunix.cl.msu.edu:80/weather/

The Electronic Frontier Foundation

The Electronic Frontier Foundation is a nonprofit civil liberties public interest organization working to protect freedom of expression, privacy and access to online resources and information. For serious discussions of these developing issues, see their page at:
http://www.eff.org/

Paris

A perfect companion to Le WebLouvre, this is a complete visitor's guide to Paris—its museums, monuments, special expositions, cafes, restaurants and sights, as well as practical information like air and rail transportation, the metro and hotels. Lots of swell images.
http://meteora.ucsd.edu:80/~norman/paris/

Sliding Tiles Puzzles

Remember those little handheld sliding tile puzzles? Here's the computer version, a collection which includes basic geometrics and celebrity faces. The sliding tile problem seems to be very popular on the net.
http://www.cm.cf.ac.uk/User/Andrew.Wilson/Puzzle/collection.html

The Virtual Radio

Hear the latest in new music here. Choose which song you'd like to hear and download it right to your machine in a radio-quality broadcast of the entire cut. Each page contains band information, a description of the music, and sometimes images of the band. Beware: with names like the Guttersluts, Fire Rooster and Metallingus, this is not marshmallow music.
http://www.microserve.net:80/vradio/

Fairy Tales

Not an HTML document, but a wonderful repository where you can download the complete text of your favorite fairy tales—Aladdin, Beauty and the Beast, Ali Baba and the Forty Thieves, The Emperor's New Clothes, Hansel and Gretel, The Pied Piper of Hamelin, The Seven Voyages of Sinbad, and other stories you've forgotten about for years. **gopher://ftp.std.com:70/11/obi/book/Fairy.Tales/Grimm**

alt.binaries Made EZ

Every day brings a hundred or so new pieces of computer art, from space pictures to "my wife streaking a hotel corridor" (we're not making this up, folks). Even if you have one of the super newsreaders that downloads and uudecodes them hands-off, the problem still is deciding what's worth your time. This French Web page provides a buffet of all the latest, on a pick 'n' click basis. **http://web.cnam.fr/Images/Usenet/**

Icon Browsers

There are so many icon browsers out there that we are forced to suspect that it's one of the tasks comp. sci. professors give their promising students as a UNIX programming exercise. Who cares? The results are greatly beneficial to the Web community at large. Copyright be damned—what's the point of 100,000 of us all laboring to create the same arrows and buttons? Here's our current favorite: **http://www.di.unipi.it/iconbrowser/icons.html**

The Global Village Idiot

There had to be one, didn't there? The Idiot claims to be "a welcome break from the Propeller-Heads that inhabit the majority of the Net" and warns that "if you have come here for Intellectual Challenge or Thoughtful Discourse, you are in the wrong place." Meet other villagers, visit the village shoppes and even dress like the Idiot.
http://www.primenet.com/~hanibal/index.html

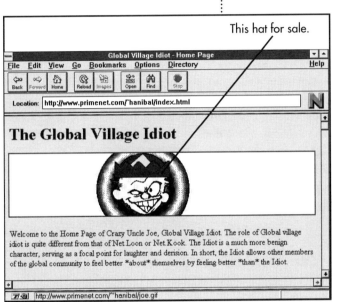

This hat for sale.

Figure 6-7: *Light relief.*

URouLette

Don't know where you want to go? Let URouLette choose for you. Spin the wheel and you'll be sent off to a random Web address. No guarantees.
http://ukanaix.cc.ukans.edu:80/cwis/organizations/ kucia/uroulette/uroulette.html

Moving On

What does the future hold on the Web? Right now it's anyone's guess. A few things are certain: the Web will get bigger, it will be easier to access, and a lot more people will be participating in it. But lots of things are unknown. Who will pay for its development? How much will it all cost? What kind of big businesses will grow out of it? How will it affect our lives—will it expand our horizons at the cost of a sense of local community?

Businesses large and small, academic institutions and governments will all have a say in this, but so will each one of us who uses it. The Internet continues to be the most revolutionary democratic forum to come along in hundreds of years.

Now that you've learned to navigate the World Wide Web with Netscape, you qualify as a fully endowed cybercitizen. Care to venture an opinion?

APPENDIX A
UNDOCUMENTED NETSCAPE FEATURES

Whether "undocumented features" are undocumented because some-body forgot to mention some brilliant piece of code to the technical writing department, or because nobody thought we'd be interested, is a matter of debate. The fact is that all software has a few features that aren't noted in the manual. Netscape is too new for a complete list to exist, but here are some we've discovered or heard about on the Netscape grapevine. The first on the list is a feature that was useful during development and never intended for release.

Browsing Your Directory

Create a file in your Netscape Navigator directory called #**FILE.HTM**. The content of this file can be anything you choose—it doesn't matter. Now start Netscape and Open #FILE.HTM as a local file, as though for HTML editing. You'll find your entire directory opens into the Netscape window, with file types identified by icons exactly as they are at an FTP site. You can click on an HTML file to load it—a very useful mode for a quick look at file content.

This mode can even be incorporated in a link like this:

<A HREF="file:///c | /netscape/# file.htm">link object</A>

A click on "link object" will then bring up your directory.

Inserting a Signature File

Insert in your NETSCAPE.INI file, in the [User] section, this statement:

sig_file=<.....path to your e-mail sig file....>

Netscape will append your sig to outgoing mail but *not* to newsgroup postings.

Different Strokes for Different Folks

These are keyboard alternatives for common commands:

Backspace acts like PgUp.

Spacebar acts like PgDn.

Ctrl-U acts like Ctrl-L to bring up the Location dialog box.

Ctrl-P launches Print mode, although the File pull-down does not indicate it.

Ctrl-C or Ctrl-Ins performs an Edit/Copy.

Ctrl-V or Shift-Ins performs an Edit/Paste.

Ctrl-X or Shift-Del performs an Edit/Cut.

What Does the N Do?

The logo is an active link: click on it and go to the Netscape Communications Corporation home page.

Who Was That Masked Programmer?

The pseudo-URL "about:" does a few interesting things—the most interesting being the form "about: authors" which brings you a list of Netscape programmers, indicating roughly who did what. We assume Lou Montulli was left on his own in the lab one night, because Netscape also reacts to the URL "montulli:"

Netscape's House Organ

The URL **http://home.mcom.com/people/** brings Netscape Communications Corporation's staff list into your content window. Many of them have home pages you can browse, and practically all have clickable mail links. You can even offer a contribution to Netscape's internal zine.

Multiple User .INI Files

Multiple users of Netscape can all have their individual NETSCAPE.INI files. To run Netscape with an .INI other than the default, create a second Netscape program item on your desktop (you can call it "Jenny's Netscape" or what you will) with the New Program Item option in the File menu. In the command line, type:

netscape -i c:\\<path to personal .INI>

Drag & Drop Netscape

You can drag a file (such as an .HTM source file) from your file manager window and drop it into Netscape. It will run.

GIF Retrieval

Browse the *.MOZ files in your cache subdirectory. Some of them will have a GIF87A header. These are images which Netscape saved in your temporary directory. Rename them as .GIF files to save them permanently.

Hypertext Newsgroup Reading

Certain versions of Netscape have no View All Newsgroups button (as depicted in Figure 4-15). You can nevertheless produce the big newsgroup file by entering **news:*** in the URL window. The newsgroup names come up as hypertext links enabling you to go to any group you like the look of. Or you can copy a newsgroup name onto the Clipboard, then paste it into the "Subscribe" window.

APPENDIX B
COMMON NETSCAPE ERROR MESSAGES

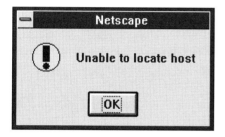

Unable to locate host

This can arise from an erroneous URL, a disconnect or the absence (perhaps temporary) of the requested site. Check your URL carefully.

Not Found

The requested object does not exist on this server. The link you followed is either outdated, inaccurate, or the server has been instructed not to let you have it. Please inform the site administrator of the referring page.

Not Found

This error comes up when you follow a link to a URL that no longer exists.

404 Not Found

The requested URL /cat/conan/gene-linkage.html was not found on this server.

404 Not Found

The URL you have provided does not exist. Check the spelling and syntax carefully.

Helper Application Not Found

Your Preferences Helper Applications dialog box refers to a helper that Netscape cannot locate in your computer. This error is thrown up when you are attempting to download a file of the type handled by the helper. Note the extension of the file you're downloading and go to the dialog box to see what Netscape is trying to find.

403 Forbidden

You're trying to visit a Web site that you or your server has no permission to access.

Connection Refused by Host

Although this one sounds the same as "Forbidden," it's more likely to be a temporary refusal. What it's saying is that the host address does actually exist, but it's not available right now. Down for maintenance, most likely—try later.

File contains no data

The URL you requested has been found but it is null. This error can sometimes be remedied by appending the port number ":80"

Too many users

You've hit a very popular site that has the maximum allowable number of visitors already.

Too many users are connected to this server

Bad File Request

This arises when you submit a form that is in some way invalid. It can also arise from erroneous HTML coding at the site you are on. Not much you can do about that!

TCP error encountered while sending request to server

Network data error. Try later. If persistent, contact your sysadmin.

Failed DNS lookup

The DNS software at your access provider's site was not able to convert a URL you requested to a valid IP address. Check the spelling and format of the URL.

NNTP Server error

Make sure you have the NNTP host entered correctly in the Preferences dialog box. If the NNTP host is correct, most likely your news server is down or congested. Try later.

Cannot add form submission result to bookmark list

When you submit a form page and get an answer page back—as, for example, when you use a web crawler to search for a keyword—the answer page is not a legitimate URL and so cannot be made into a bookmark. Look at the URL string and somewhere you'll see "cgi-bin." Any time you see that as part of a URL you'll know this is a nonsavable answer page.

GLOSSARY

Alias A type of nickname used, for example, in e-mail managers so that you can enter "fred" and your e-mail manager knows you mean "edf556@froward.cursci.com".

Anchor In hypertext, the object that is highlighted and "clickable." It may be a word, a phrase, or an inline image.

Anonymous FTP An FTP service that serves any user, not just users having accounts at the site. Anonymous FTP generally permits downloading of all files, but uploading only into a directory called "/incoming."

Archie A keyword search service that searches the directory and file titles of all FTP sites that are indexed.

ASCII (American Standard Code for Information Interchange) An agreed-upon coding of letters, numbers and symbols. An ASCII file is one which makes use of only the first 128 ASCII symbols—the symbols you see on your keyboard, basically. The advantage of ASCII files is that one bit per byte is always available for purposes such as error-checking.

.AU In hypermedia, an audio file format common in DOS systems.

Backbone   The connections between the primary computers in a network. Stub networks branch off the backbone.

Bandwidth   Used (somewhat inaccurately) to express the maximum possible throughput of a data link in bits per second. A so-called T1 line has a bandwidth of 1.544 Mbps.

Binary   A numbering system used in computing, which has two as its base. A binary file, as opposed to an ASCII file, makes use of 256 symbols and so does not keep a bit free for error-checking.

Bookmark   A Web address in the form of a URL that a user keeps a record of in order to be able to return to it easily.

Cache   1. An area of RAM set aside to hold data or instructions that would normally be read from disk, in order to speed up access to it. 2. In network operation, an area of disk set aside to hold data that would normally be read from the Net, for the same reason. Netscape makes use of both types of cache.

Chameleon   A commercial Internet package designed specifically for the Windows environment by NetManage of Cupertino, CA.

Client/server software   An arrangement of computers, very common in Internet systems, whereby a small system called the client makes use of the data management services of a much larger computer, the server. Netscape Navigator is a client/server system, with the client running on your machine taking advantage of the far greater processing power of the server at a remote site.

Content window   The portion of the Netscape screen in which actual page content is seen, as opposed to the control and information portions.

Cyberspace   Fanciful term coined by William Gibson in the novel *Neuromancer* to describe the sum total of computer-accessible information in the world.

Dial-up account   The type of Internet access account that is connected only when a modem connection is established, as distinct from a direct permanent connection. Often used to refer to a shell account as opposed to a SLIP or PPP-type access, even though SLIP/PPP accounts are frequently also established by dialup.

Direct connection   A hard-wired connection between a computer and the Internet, giving the computer an IP address and the ability to function as a Web site.

DNS (Domain Name Server)   Software that converts host names to IP addresses.

Eudora   A popular e-mail manager developed by Qualcomm Inc. of San Diego.

.EXE file extension   In DOS, denotes an "executable" file that will run if its name is simply entered at the DOS prompt (with or without the .EXE). Files that are executable in Windows frequently have the extension .EXE also.

External image   An image that may be accessed by a hypertext link from an HTML page, but is not automatically displayed when the page loads, as is an in-line image.

FAQ (Frequently Asked Questions) Pronounced FAK, shorthand for an information file about some system. In USENET newsgroups, you should always read any FAQs you can find because if you ask a question that's already covered in the FAQ you are likely to be "flamed" (see below).

Finger Originally a UNIX command requesting information about another registered UNIX account-holder. Now available to Netscape by courtesy of Finger "gateways."

Flame A deliberately abusive message in e-mail or USENET post.

FTP (File Transfer Protocol) One of the original protocols on the Internet, which allows for very efficient transfer of entire data files between computers but discourages interactive browsing.

.GIF (Graphics Interchange Format) One of many formats for computerized images, designed to be highly transportable between computer systems. Almost invariably used for in-line images in Web pages.

Gopher An Internet search-and-display application that reduces all Internet resource "trees" to onscreen menus.

Greek In desktop publishing, an approximate representation of text used when there is insufficient screen space to show it in properly readable form. By extension, any onscreen text that is garbled.

Helper applications Applications that cooperate with Netscape and other Web browsers to perform functions that Netscape itself is not programmed to perform, such as viewing video files.

Home page   1. Whatever page you designate (in the Preferences/Styles dialog box) as the Web page you want Netscape to load at startup. 2. A personal page you control and refer other people to.

Host   A computer whose primary function is facilitating communications.

Hotlist   A personal list of favorite Web addresses, organized so that it creates hypertext links to the addresses. Same as a bookmark list.

HTML (HyperText Markup Language)   A convention for inserting "tags" into a text file that Web browsers like Netscape can interpret to display or link to hypermedia. HTML files usually have the extension .HTML or .HTM.

HTML+   A more rigorous version of HTML, allowing for a wider range of media effects.

Hypermedia   Media such as video and audio, which go beyond what was thought (not so very long ago!) to be the realm of personal computer display.

Hypertext   System of interactive text linking allowing the reader to choose any path through the sum total of available text.

In-line image   On a Web page, an image to be loaded along with the page text (although in-lines can be suppressed by a Netscape user to speed up page-loading).

Internet   A network of computer networks stretching across the world, linking computers of many different types. No one organization has control of the Internet or jurisdiction over it.

IP address   An Internet machine address formatted with numbers rather than a host name. An IP address may also contain a port number, separated from the host address by a colon.

.JPEG (Joint Photographic Experts Group)   A modern image file format allowing for a choice of three levels of file compression, with progressive trade-off of image quality.

Killer app   A highly acclaimed successful and popular computer application.

Link   In the World Wide Web context, short for "hypertext link," meaning a path a user may follow that connects one part of a document to another part of the same document, a different document or some other resource.

Lynx   Name of a text-only World Wide Web browser, available for UNIX, Linux, DOS and a few other operating systems.

Mail server   A computer whose primary function is e-mail management for a group of subscribers.

MIME (Multipurpose Internet Mail Extensions)   A set of agreed-upon formats enabling binary files to be sent as e-mail or attached to e-mail. "MIME types" have come to mean hypermedia formats in general, even when not communicated by e-mail.

Mirror site   A subsidiary FTP site that has the same content as the main site that it reflects. Used to take the load off sites so popular that they are frequently inaccessible because of congestion.

Mosaic   A World Wide Web graphical browser, forerunner of Netscape Navigator.

Mozilla   Pet name the software authors gave to Netscape Navigator during development, which has survived as the name of the green monster who decorates many of the Netscape information pages.

.MPEG (Motion Picture Experts Group)   Modern standard format for compression and storage of video hypermedia files.

NCSA (National Center for Supercomputing Applications)   A U.S. Government center at the University of Illinois. NCSA developed the Mosaic Web browser and other Internet interfaces.

NEWSRC file   Data file that keeps a record of which newsgroups a user is subscribed to, and which articles have already been read.

Newsreader   Software whose function is to interact with USENET newsgroups, providing services such as subscription, display, follow-up, print, download and so on.

Newt   The TCP/IP part of Chameleon. Newt can be used to establish a SLIP or PPP Internet connection for Netscape.

NNTP (Network News Transport Protocol)   The protocol used by the USENET newsgroups to disseminate bulletins.

Packet-switching A system, used extensively throughout the Internet, for handling messages based upon the breakdown of a message into standardized packets, each of which is independently routed to the addressee.

POP mail (Post Office Protocol) An e-mail system that establishes your primary mailbox in your own desktop computer rather than at your access provider's site.

PPP (Point-to-Point Protocol) A convention for transmitting packet-switched data.

Proxy A device used to access the Internet around a "fire wall" put up to ensure security in a large system.

QuickTime A hypermedia video format, invented for Macintosh multimedia systems but now also available for DOS/Windows.

Search engine Keyword searching algorithm or complete software package including search algorithms.

Server The server half of a client/server pair: the computer that handles the primary data management tasks on behalf of its clients.

Shell A simple, usually menu-driven, interface that shields a computer user from the complexities of operating systems such as UNIX. Hence a common type of Internet connection, known as a "UNIX shell account," can be operated efficiently with extremely limited actual knowledge of UNIX.

SLIP (Serial Line Internet Protocol)   A convention for transmitting packet-switched data.

Socket   One of a series of memory addresses in a computer reserved for data exchange with a TCP/IP stack.

Source document   In the World Wide Web, the raw file that an HTML author creates, as distinct from a Web page which is the representation of a source document in hypertext.

Stack   In the context of TCP/IP, the ordered series of protocols and packet drivers required to interface a desktop computer with the Internet.

Tag   Name given to the code strings embedded in HTML documents, such as <H1>.

TCP/IP (Transmission Control Protocol/Internet Protocol)   Shorthand for the most common packet-switching protocols used on the Internet.

TELNET   A software system that establishes a connection between two computers for the purpose of data exchange. Unlike FTP, TELNET is interactive and, as commonly used, makes a desktop computer behave as though it were the workstation of a much larger computer.

.TIFF (Tagged Image File Format)   A standard format for storing hypermedia image files. A .TIFF file is uncompressed (and therefore generally large) and can contain many images.

Trumpet Winsock   A popular Winsock package (TCP/IP stack) designed by Peter Tattam of the University of Tasmania. (See also Winsock.)

UNIX   The operating system of choice for computers dedicated to the Internet. UNIX is inherently suited to network operations.

URL (Universal Resource Locator)   An address that completely defines a resource of the World Wide Web. A URL has four elements:

1. The service—http or ftp or a few others.
2. The host—the computer that handles the resource.
3. The port number (often not necessary because it defaults according to the service requested).
4. The path and filename of the resource.

Format of a URL is service://host:port/path.

USENET   A worldwide network exchanging news bulletins grouped under subject categories called "newsgroups." Most newsgroups are open, and anyone may contribute. Netscape has its own built-in newsreader for interacting with USENET. (See also Newsreader.)

WAIS (Wide Area Information Service)   A database service of the Internet allowing structured searching for keyword combinations. WAIS supplies a measure of how well documents it finds match your keywords in the form of a "relevance score," with a score of 1000 being a perfect match.

.WAV   A standard format for storing hypermedia audio files.

Web   Short for the World Wide Web.

Web browser   User interface to the Web. Netscape is a graphical Web browser.

Web crawler   Software that searches the Web (or, more commonly, a database *derived* from the Web) for keywords input by a user.

Web page   Coherent document that is readable by a Web browser. A Web page may vary in complexity all the way from a simple piece of text enclosed by the HTML tags <PRE>....</PRE>, meaning "pre-formatted," to a densely coded HTML file giving the user access to many types of hypermedia.

Web server   A server computer equipped to offer World Wide Web access to its clients.

Web spider   A type of keyword search software.

Webmaster   Person at a Web server site who is qualified to administer all Web resources at that site.

Winsock   Short for Windows Sockets: the interface between your Windows version of Netscape Navigator and the TCP/IP stack you are running.

World Wide Web   Arrangement of Internet-accessible resources, including hypertext and hypermedia, addressed by URLs.

Zine   Any online magazine.

INDEX

S

T

U

V

COLOPHON

This book was developed on a Power Macintosh 8100/80. All pages were produced in Aldus PageMaker 5.0. Some graphics were edited in Photoshop 3.0. Proof copies were printed on a Hewlett-Packard LaserJet 4M Plus.

Chapter titles are set in Anna. Chapter numbers are set in Futura Condensed Bold. The body text is Palatino with Futura Heavy subheads. Tables and sidebars are set in Futura. The title of the book (on the cover and also on the title pages) is set in Michelangelo.

Internet Resources

The Windows Internet Tour Guide, Second Edition
$29.95, 424 pages, illustrated

Users can now navigate the Internet the easy way: by pointing and clicking, dragging and dropping. In easy-to-read, entertaining prose, the *Windows Internet Tour Guide* leads you through installing and using the software enclosed in the book to send and receive e-mail, transfer files, search the Internet's vast resources and more! **BONUS**: Free trial access and two free electronic updates.

Internet E-Mail Quick Tour
$14.00, 152 pages, illustrated

Whether it's the Internet or an online service, most people use their connections primarily for electronic messaging. This all-in-one guide to getting it right includes tips on software, security, style and Netiquette. Also included: how to obtain an e-mail account, useful addresses, interesting mailing lists and more!

Publishing on the Internet, Windows Edition
$34.95, 400 pages, illustrated

Successful publishing for the Internet requires an understanding of "nonlinear" presentation as well as specialized software. Both are here. Learn how HTML builds the hot links that let readers choose their own paths—and how to use effective design to drive a message or theme. The companion CD-ROM contains Ventana Mosaic™, an HTML editor, a graphics viewer, templates, conversion software and more. Available in April.

Internet Virtual Worlds Quick Tour

$14.00, 150 pages, illustrated

Learn to locate and master real-time interactive communication forums and games by participating in the virtual worlds of MUD (Multi-User Dimension) and MOO (MUD Object-Oriented). *Internet Virtual Worlds Quick Tour* introduces users to the basic functions by defining different categories (individual, interactive and both) and detailing standard protocols. Also revealed is the insider's lexicon of these mysterious cyberworlds. Available in March.

Internet Roadside Attractions

$29.95, 384 pages, illustrated

Why take the word of one when you can get a quorum? Seven experienced Internauts—teachers and bestselling authors—share their favorite Web sites, Gophers, FTP sites, chats, games, newsgroups and mailing lists. Organized alphabetically by category for easy browsing with in-depth descriptions. The companion CD-ROM contains the entire text of the book, hyperlinked for off-line browsing and online Web-hopping.

Internet Chat Quick Tour

$14.00, 200 pages, illustrated

The first eyewitness reports of the USSR's demise came not from radio but the Internet! Discover how worldwide chat networks are changing the way we communicate, with live help forums, discussion groups, performing arts and more. An inside look at chat software includes sources, how-to's and tips on locating chat servers. Available in March.

Books marked with this logo include a free Internet *Online Companion*™, featuring archives of free utilities plus a software archive and links to other Internet resources.

Insightful Guides

The Official America Online for Windows Membership Kit & Tour Guide, Second Edition

$27.95, 568 pages, illustrated

Experience the delights of online communications and AOL's easy graphical interface. The second edition of this bestseller offers a glimpse of AOL's fresh new interface, reorganized services and Internet access. Tips on saving time and money online are liberally spiced with behind-the-scenes stories and online experiences. The companion disk includes the latest version of AOL's starter software, one month free membership and 20 hours of free online time (new members only).

America Online's Internet, Windows Edition

$24.95, 328 pages, illustrated

AOL members can now slide onto the Infobahn with a mere mouse click. This quick-start for AOL Internet newcomers explains e-mail, downloading files, reading newsgroups and joining mailing lists. The companion disk includes AOL software and ten hours of free online time (for new members only).

Voodoo Windows

$19.95, 312 pages, illustrated

Work Windows wizardry with productivity-enhancing tips. Organized by subject, this book offers a wealth of Windows techniques, shortcuts and never-before-published tricks that will streamline your daily tasks and save time. A great reference for beginners and experienced users alike.

Windows, Word & Excel Office Companion, Second Edition
$21.95, 694 pages, illustrated

With more than 100,000 copies sold, this groundbreaking title eliminates the need for newcomers to purchase three separate books. Three sections offer easy introductions to Microsoft's industry-leading software: Windows™ through Version 3.1, Word through Version 6 and Excel through Version 5. An extensive index makes this down-to-earth guide to basic commands and features an easy reference that saves time, money and valuable desktop acreage.

The Windows Shareware 500
$39.95, 456 pages, illustrated

The best Windows shareware available, from thousands of contenders. Includes utilities, sounds, fonts, icons, games, clip art, multimedia and more. **BONUS:** Four companion disks: three that feature top-rated programs and an America Online membership disk. Includes 10 hours free online time (for new members only).

The Visual Guide to Paradox for Windows
$29.95, 692 pages, illustrated

A uniquely pictorial approach to Paradox! Hundreds of examples and illustrations show how to achieve complex database development with simple drag-and-drop techniques. Users learn how to access and modify database files, use Form and Report Designers and Experts, program with ObjectPal and more—all with icons, buttons, graphics and OLE. The companion disk contains sample macros, forms, reports, tables, queries and a ready-to-use database.

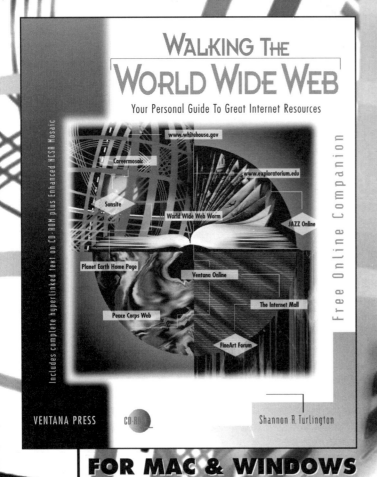

WALKING THE WORLD WIDE WEB

Your Personal Guide To Great Internet Resources

Includes complete hyperlinked text on CD-ROM plus Enhanced NCSA Mosaic

Free Online Companion

VENTANA PRESS

CD-ROM

Shannon R. Turlington

FOR MAC & WINDOWS

Walk the Web!

Tour the best of the best. Shannon Turlington takes you on a memorable trip to more than 300 exciting Web sites. With in-depth descriptions of why each one is special, Turlington shows how easy it is to visit and enjoy these innovative, engaging and informative sites!

Full text on CD-ROM—browse at your leisure off-line. Then when you've plotted your trip, log on and use this hyperlinked version of *Walking the World Wide Web* to point and click your way to the world's most exciting sites.

Free! One-year subscription to *Online Companion*™—a full online version of *Walking the World Wide Web* residing on Ventana Online™, featuring updates and new additions regularly—**a $19.95 value!**

Ventana Online also provides free instant access to the latest versions of all the free software mentioned in *Walking the World Wide Web*—including updates and change notes, the moment they are available. All with point-and-click convenience, in a friendly format for Mac and Windows.

$29.95, 360 pages, illustrated.

TITLE	ISBN	Quantity		Price		Total
America Online's Internet, Windows Version	1-56604-176-7	_____	x	$24.95	=	$_____
Internet Chat Quick Tour	1-56604-223-2	_____	x	$14.00	=	$_____
Internet E-Mail Quick Tour	1-56604-220-8	_____	x	$14.00	=	$_____
Internet Roadside Attractions	1-56604-193-7	_____	x	$29.95	=	$_____
Internet Virtual Worlds Quick Tour	1-56604-222-4	_____	x	$14.00	=	$_____
The Official America Online For Windows Membership Kit & Tour Guide, 2nd Edition	1-56604-128-7	_____	x	$27.95	=	$_____
Publishing on the Internet, Windows Edition	1-56604-229-1	_____	x	$34.95	=	$_____
The Visual Guide to Paradox for Windows	1-56604-150-3	_____	x	$29.95	=	$_____
Voodoo Windows	1-56604-005-1	_____	x	$19.95	=	$_____
Walking the World Wide Web	1-56604-208-9	_____	x	$29.95	=	$_____
The Windows Internet Tour Guide, 2nd Edition	1-56604-174-0	_____	x	$29.95	=	$_____
The Windows Shareware 500	1-56604-045-0	_____	x	$39.95	=	$_____
Windows, Word & Excel Office Companion, 2nd Edition	1-56604-083-3	_____	x	$21.95	=	$_____
				Subtotal	=	$_____
				Shipping	=	$_____
				TOTAL	=	$_____

To order any Ventana Press title, complete this order form and mail or fax it to us, with payment, for quick shipment.

SHIPPING:

For all standard orders, please ADD $4.50/first book, $1.35/each additional.
For "two-day air," ADD $8.25/first book, $2.25/each additional.
For orders to Canada, ADD $6.50/book.
For orders sent C.O.D., ADD $4.50 to your shipping rate.
North Carolina residents must ADD 6% sales tax.
International orders require additional shipping charges.

Name _____ Daytime telephone _____

Company _____

Address (No PO Box) _____

City_____ State_____ Zip _____

___ Payment enclosed ___VISA ___ MC Acc't # _____ Exp. date_____

Exact name on card _____ Signature _____

Check your local bookstore or software retailer for these and other bestselling titles, or call toll free 800/743-5369

Mail to: Ventana Press, PO Box 2468, Chapel Hill, NC 27515 ☎ 800/743-5369 Fax 919/942-1140

ABOUT THE ONLINE COMPANION

Netscape into the World Wide Web! The *Netscape Online Companion* is an informative tool, as well as an annotated software library. It aids in your exploration of the World Wide Web while at the same time supporting and enhancing the Netscape Web Browser. Sections of *Netscape Quick Tour,* the hard copy book, are reproduced and hyperlinked to the exciting WWW sites and tools that they reference. So you can just click on the name of the reference and jump directly to the site you are intercepted in.

Perhaps one of the most impressive features of the *Netscape Online Companion* is its Software Archive. Here, you'll find and be able to download the latest versions of all the software mentioned in *Netscape Quick Tour* that are freely available on the Internet. This software ranges from Netscape helper applications such as Mpeg Player, SoundMachine and Wham, which enhance Netscape's graphics and sound capabilities to many of your basic Internet essentials such as Eudora, an e-mail tool, and Fetch, which allows

you to easily transfer files to and from your computer. Also with Ventana Online's helpful description of the software you'll know exactly what you're getting and why. So you won't download the software just to find you have no use for it.

The *Netscape Online Companion* also links you to the Ventana Library where you will find useful press and jacket information on a variety of Ventana Press offerings. Plus, you have access to a wide selection of exciting new releases and coming attractions. In addition, Ventana's Online Library allows you to order the books you want.

The *Netscape Online Companion* represents Ventana Online's ongoing commitment to offering the most dynamic and exciting products possible. And soon Ventana Online will be adding more services, including more multimedia supplements, searchable indices and sections of the book reproduced and hyperlinked to the Internet resources they reference.

To access, connect via the World Wide Web to **http://www.vmedia.com/nqt.html**